GREAT WOMEN OF FILM

GREAT WOMEN OF FILM
HELENA LUMME

PHOTOGRAPHS BY
MIKA MANNINEN
& HELENA LUMME

BILLBOARD BOOKS
AN IMPRINT OF WATSON-GUPTILL PUBLICATIONS / NEW YORK

Page 5 photo of Ruth Carter; Page 6 of Teri Dorman;
Page 8 of Vicky Jenson, Lorna Cook, Brenda Chapman

Senior Acquisitions Editor: Bob Nirkind
Editor: Gabrielle Pecarsky
Designer: Steve Mortensen
Production Manager: Ellen Greene

First published in 2002 by Billboard Books
an imprint of Watson-Guptill Publications,
a division of VNU Business Media, Inc.
770 Broadway, New York, NY 10003
www.watsonguptill.com

Library of Congress Cataloging-in-Publication Data

Lumme, Helena,
  Great women of Film / Helena Lumme ; photographs by Mika Manninen &
Helena Lumme.
     p. cm.
  ISBN 0-8230-7956-2
  1. Women in the motion picture industry. I. Manninen, Mika, II.
Title.
  PN1998.2 .L86 2002
  384'.8'082--dc21

                              2001005372

Printed in the United States

First printing, 2002

1 2 3 4 5 6 7 8 9/08 07 06 05 04 03 02

For filmmakers, film lovers, and all eternal film students.

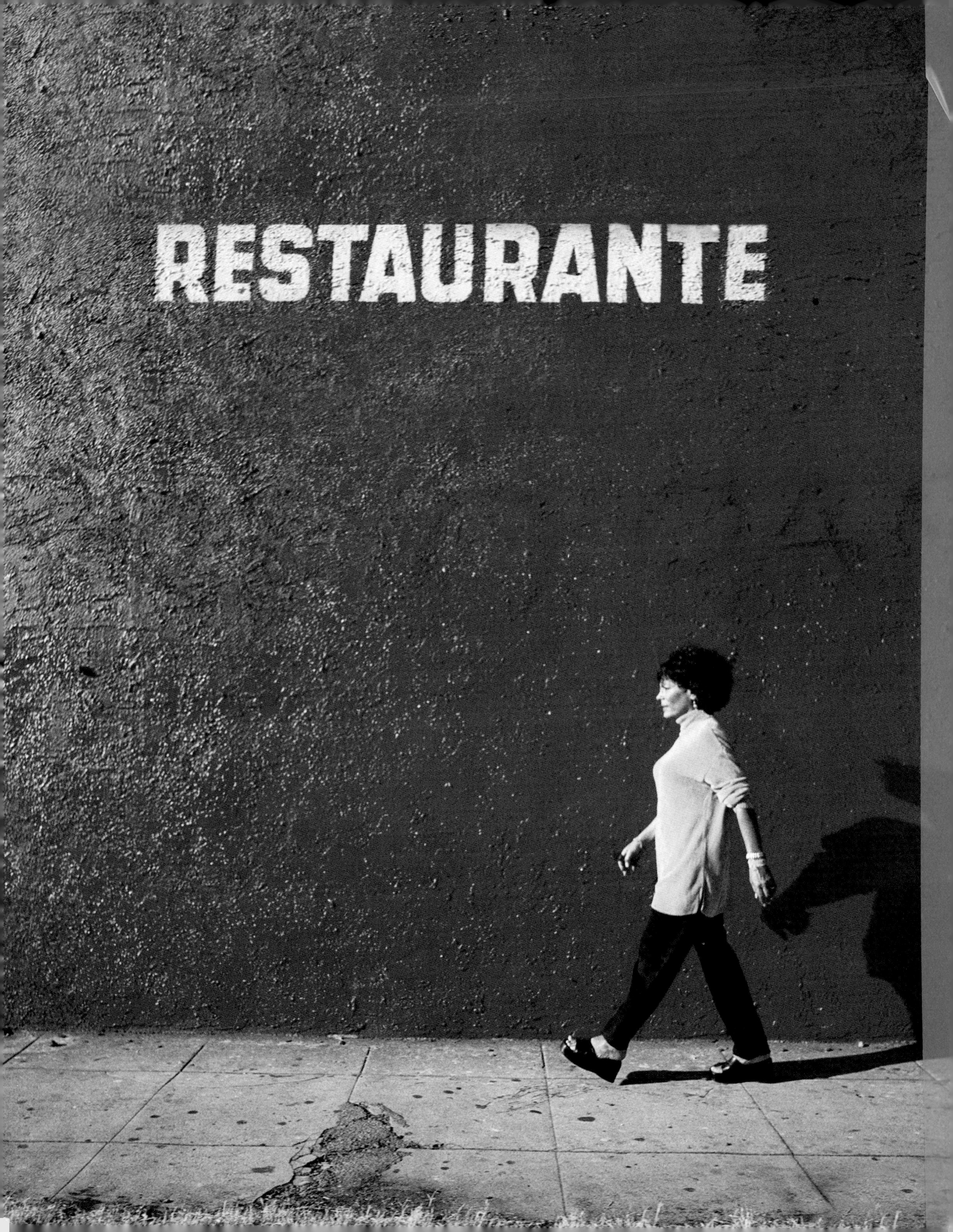
RESTAURANTE

CONTENTS

This book is a celebration of excellence in the craft of moviemaking.

For those who want to know more about how movies are made, and about the people and skills needed to bring magic to our screens;

For those who are considering a career in film and want to find out about the dream jobs beyond directing and acting;

For anyone who wonders what it takes to make it to the top and stay there;

This illustrated tour of moviemaking is narrated by those who created their own luck, and are generous enough to share their stories.

The fact that they all happen to be women is—like everything else in Hollywood—pure coincidence.

Helena Lumme

ROBIN SWICORD
SCREENWRITER

All of us have the time. Few have the obsession.

I DIDN'T KNOW that films were written.

Growing up in a small town in the South, I thought that authors wrote books, and actors and directors made up the movies. I was going to be an author. During summer vacation, I wrote a "chapter book" about a heroic ballerina/detective/witch who went back in time to pioneer days and saved her family. In the slow afternoons at school, I covered notebook paper with what I later realized were "storyboards"—pages gridded with boxes, with crude drawings of people and dialogue in each box. A college professor encouraged me to write autobiographical short stories in a literary "Southern absurd" voice. I loved literature, but I also enjoyed the forbidden pleasures that fell far outside the academic sphere: glossy Hollywood romances with Audrey Hepburn, 16mm experimental films featuring Rip Torn, old B-movies about Tarzan falling into a pit of snakes or teenagers surfing and dating. I liked comic books, stage plays, Broadway musicals, Spanish foto-novelas, Julie Andrews, and, in fact, all music rather indiscriminately, from Sonny Terry's scratchy blues to Tom Lehrer parodies.

I was a current-events junkie—I worked crummy jobs in newsrooms mostly for the human interest stories that spewed in endless miles from the teletype machine: conspiracy theorists and airplane hobbyists and ex-cons trying to clear their names and mothers who had drowned their children. I devoured images: Robert Frank, Diane Arbus, Walker Evans, Cartier Bresson. For no reason at all, I collected postcards: thousands of bathing beauties, farm trucks carrying giant Idaho potatoes, Seminoles wrestling alligators, eerily bland motel rooms. At the library, I pored over old fashion photographs, lusting after clothes by Balenciaga, Dior, Schiaparelli. When I was supposed to be researching, I read magazines: *Architectural Digest* for its incredible rooms like stage sets, *National Geographic* for the saturated colors and tribal costumes, the library's entire archive of *LIFE,* cover to cover, which gave me the twentieth century in pictures. I obsessed over daily comics (and still do), cutting out single frames from narrative strips like *Brenda Starr, Rex Morgan MD, Mary Worth,* and *Apt. 3-G.*

Socially, I was a spy and an eavesdropper, a diviner of secrets, a cold-hearted analyst, a consumer of human behavior. To the disappointment of teachers who thought I had some writing ability, what I turned out to be was a dramatist.

The horrible thing about writing drama is that you invariably write badly at first. Drama is hard. Letters, novels, short stories, and even some poems are, at a rudimentary level, composed of simple declarative sentences that convey information in a comprehensible order. Given sufficient will, patience, and a good editor, any capable writer should be able to turn out at least one passable example. Screenplays are more exacting. To be even medium-good, a screenplay must have the concision of poetry, the visual power of a folio of photographs, the compression and detail of a short story, the narrative drive and thematic underpinnings of a novel, dialogue that sounds like human speech only better, characters who fascinate, and a particular idiosyncratic juxtaposition of events that create a structure we viscerally recognize as being "dramatic."

This isn't to say we shouldn't try.

My favorite *New Yorker* cartoon shows a happy fellow in a sporty jacket at a cocktail party, who says to a baggy-eyed, haunted-looking man who clutches a drink: "You're a writer? I've always wanted to write, but I've never had the time."

All of us have the time. Few have the obsession.

If you're willing to sit in a chair and put words on paper *every* day—not just occasionally or when you are "inspired," but every day—and you do this for a number of years (I don't know how many), you will find out whether you can write. At first you force yourself to the daily discipline of putting words on the page. After a duration, obsession takes over. Eventually (if you're a writer) you'll become the baggy-eyed, haunted person at the party, inattentively listening to this fellow in his fashionable jacket, while your mind wanders back to that unfinished scene waiting for you on your desk.

The wonderful thing about writing drama is that not only are you literally the first person to see the movie, but you play all of the parts. If a camera hidden in your ceiling would reveal you to be an insane person who paces around your desk maniacally repeating certain lines aloud to no one, trying out different inflections, if you erupt into sudden laughter or hunch over your computer keyboard in tears, if your face contorts into rage or you flinch from a blow— you're probably doing something right.

Writing drama means collaborating. Your initial coconspirator is usually the producer—he or she talks over ideas and may act as a kind of dramaturg, giving you advice on your early drafts of a project. A producer who can actually give you perceptive writing notes is invaluable. (Work with him/her again, if at all possible.) After each draft you meet with film executives who make useful/destructive suggestions that lead to the further refinement/full-out implosion of your screenplay. It's your job to figure out which note will lead to what. A good producer will help protect the script from bad ideas.

Rarely—statistically *very* rarely for female screenwriters—your project may move toward production. The producers and executives hire a director and then try to hire movie stars; or sometimes they hire movie stars and eventually find a director. The director might "reconceive" the project beyond recognition, or might join his/her vision to yours and genuinely strive to bring something close to your intention to the screen. Most directors do something in between. As you continue to revise, a casting director comes in to help fill out the remaining roles. The actors voice their script concerns to the producer or director, and you revise as needed. Gradually other strategists and talented artists join the company: the line producer, who manages the planning and day-to-day concerns, costumers, designers, the film editor, the composer, and so on. Soon the project is no longer "mine" but "ours"—or, in the worst of experiences, "theirs."

When creative people are well matched and share a common vision, working together to make a film is a pleasure, and all those years of writing alone on the project seem worth it. When the collaboration doesn't go well, you have to repair yourself, find your resilience, and move on with other work. The Blessing and The Curse: There's always something you must write.

Advice to beginning screenwriters: Read. Take another look at Aristotle's *Poetics*. (His observations on drama do apply to movies.) Spend some time in "virtual film school": As a regular activity, watch videos of movies *with the sound turned off.* Observe how the story unfolds, note where the editor cuts, where the next scene begins, how information is conveyed without dialogue. What do the characters' clothes tell us? What about the set dressing? Think about the people: What makes a character The Protagonist? How does the writer seduce the viewer into wanting to be represented by this Protagonist?

Replay the movie in your head scene by scene and think about cause and effect. How do the scenes "push" each other, each causing the next to happen? Become alert to structure: How do the different story strands interweave? Where does the Beginning end and the Middle begin? Where does the Middle set up the End?

With the sound on, study an individual scene. What are the elements that contribute to an emotional moment? Every detail in a scene represents a choice that someone made. How would the scene change if the actor played it another way or were wearing different clothes? What if the scene started earlier or ended later; if the camera were closer or farther away? What role does music play in making a moment work?

Teaching yourself to *see the craft* will help you get filmmaking under your skin, and it may shorten that period of time in which you write badly. It has one unfortunate side effect—it ruins movies for you forever. But you'll be ready to write.

Writer: Practical Magic (1998)   Matilda (1996)   The Perez Family (1995)   Little Women (1994)   The Red Coat (1994, short)   Shag (1989)   You Ruined My Life (1987, TV)
Producer: Practical Magic (1998, coproducer)   Matilda (1996, coproducer)   The Perez Family (1995, executive producer)   Little Women (1994, coproducer)
Director: The Red Coat (1994, short)

BONNIE CURTIS

PRODUCER

You can never get so focused on a little problem that you forget the bigger picture. You have 20 to 25 department heads that you are in charge of, and it's their job to deal with the minutiae. If you don't keep the big picture, no one else will.

I WANTED TO MAKE MOVIES for as long as I can remember. I really got addicted at age ten. I started begging my parents to see everything. I would go to the theaters and see five movies a day. By the time VCRs kicked in, it was movie-marathon time constantly. I went to school in Texas, at Abilene Christian University. They didn't have a film department but had a great journalism school, so I studied journalism.

I moved to L.A. in 1988. I got a job at Disney as a production assistant. I met a woman there who had worked on and off for Steven Spielberg for eight years. One day Steven called her and said, "I need an assistant. Can you help me find somebody?" I had just been promoted, so I declined. My boyfriend at the time thought I was insane. Everyone understands that when Steven Spielberg offers you a job, you take it.

Bonnie Curtis had second thoughts, so she met with Kathleen Kennedy, Spielberg's producer at Amblin.

Kathy and I hit it off immediately. I met Steven the next week and hit it off with him, too. I worked as his assistant for six years, through *Hook, Jurassic Park, Amistad,* and *Schindler's List.* After he started DreamWorks SKG with Jeffrey Katzenberg and David Geffen, I was still his assistant, although I had already done some production work. One day, I told him I couldn't do his calendar anymore, I needed to do movies. I remember him saying, "I thought I had found my Alma." I said, "Your what?" He told me that Alma was Hitchcock's assistant till he died.

It ended up being a good thing that I was working as his assistant when we were setting up DreamWorks. I got to know everyone that we hired—all the executives, all the lawyers, all the animation people— which helped me a lot when I started producing.

I became an associate producer on *The Lost World.* I got to follow Kathleen Kennedy around—I literally shadowed her for four months. I sat in every meeting with her, sat in the trailer with her, just hung out with Kathy. That was the best possible thing that could have happened to me. I learned a lot because I was sponging it but not really doing it yet. I had the time of my life every day, and I didn't feel like I was working.

WHAT PRODUCING IS ALL ABOUT

Saving Private Ryan was the film in which I really started to figure out what producing was all about. As coproducer, I saw it through from beginning to end—I was in Ireland and England for four months, and I was busy for at least another year with publicity, marketing, international release, and video. I love all that stuff: figuring out the poster, the trailer, how you're going to get people into the theater.

There are a lot of different ways to produce a movie, none of them right or wrong. And the time line varies with each movie. Like preproduction: you can do a rush-prep in 12 weeks, but you really need, for a huge movie, six months. The first *Jurassic Park* was prepped for a year. You start by putting together your art department, full-throttle prep for probably three months. If there are a lot of visual effects involved, and you're attempting to do something that's never been done before, you have to give yourself time to figure it out.

Once shooting starts, a lot of producers are maybe doing a few movies at once, so they're not on the set every day. There's usually a line producer on the set every day, or a U.P.M. (unit production manager). I like to spend about half and half: half of the time on the set, the other half in my trailer or office making calls and setting everything up for the following day.

An important rule of producing is nobody needs surprises. You have to respect how far ahead the director is prepping, and communicate early. I can walk in and say to the director, "That set we're going in on tomorrow, that wall you needed to be mirrors, well, they didn't get here in time. So here's what we're doing, okay?" But if he first walked onto that set and saw the wall wasn't a wall of mirrors, then there could be a problem. You have to let people know about changes ahead of time, and give them time to create new solutions.

Communication is key with everyone. Better to tell things too many times than too few. But how you communicate … well, that's a personality thing. I know there are people who won't respond unless I put my thoughts into writing, people I've got to send a fax to, people who will only communicate by e-mail. You learn who needs what. Then there are the people you don't have to ever talk to, they're so good. You hand them a script, you have one meeting with them, and you never have to talk to

A Day in the Life of a Producer

7:00 A.M. — Arrive on set. First and second A.D.s are waiting for me at my parking space. This is not the way I want to start the day. One of our leads has an ill child, needs to stay home today for at least half a day. Find the director. Can we shoot around? Well, we could shoot what is scheduled for tomorrow, but the set won't be ready until 10:00 A.M. Can we start lighting it? Yes. Okay, shoot as much as we can on current set without all of our actors; move to tomorrow's work.

7:10 — Head for makeup trailer. Need to check in with our star to make sure he is okay with our shift in plans.

7:15 — Call into office to go through list for the day. I still have 25 phone calls from yesterday that I need to return: agents, managers, casting directors, studio lawyers, studio clearance, and studio business people. There are still some casting decisions that need to be made for the scenes we are shooting next Tuesday. Our bluescreen unit got only half of what they needed to shoot last night because of a crane problem. Extras casting is having difficulty finding enough people for the exterior background shot on Friday, and we've run into a real dead end trying to get clearance on a poem we need in a scene next week.

7:25 — Go by caterers and grab a Dr Pepper and a quick bite to eat.

7:30 — Stage walk-through with production designer and director. Everything looks great.

8:00 — Begin shooting what we can without all our leads. In between shots, I can squeeze in a few phone calls.

10:00 — Run back to office for a meeting with the studio's advertising team. Begin heading into creative direction to pitch to director.

11:15 — Head of the studio calls. Wants to discuss the budget and schedule. Make sure my update on numbers is latest update.

1:00 P.M. — Break for lunch. Grab a plate of food and run to screening room to look at yesterday's dailies.

2:00 — Back from lunch. Shooting resumes. Return the rest of yesterday's calls.

3:40 — Meet with casting director and director between shots to go through tape on some possible actors. None of them work—now we understand what director is looking for. Back to the drawing board.

5:00 — Meet with production accountant and unit production manager to go over our cost report. We are over budget in some departments. Figure out where we can make that up or compromise.

6:00 — Director smells some sort of gas leak in corner of stage—call studio fire department! We're okay.

7:00 — Wrap shooting.

7:05 — Review tomorrow's shooting schedule with department heads and director.

8:00 — Head home.

them again. You just want to hug them because it's one less thing you have to deal with.

NUDGE, NUDGE, NUDGE

You're constantly reassessing your schedule, constantly reassessing your budget. A lot of my stuff is just nudging. Nudge, nudge, nudge. And when you are shooting for 77 days on a 160-page script for a $100 million movie, it is a pain in the ass. But it's such a process of evolution. If you look at the movie you planned to make at day one and you reassess on day 50, sometimes you're in awe of the things that ended up happening.

GETTING YOUR FOOT IN THE DOOR

My advice is go to college, and major in something that actually educates you, like history or English literature or journalism. Study something that forces you to read and write a lot. There are so many people that can't put an intelligent thought together. And good writers are desperately needed. Secondly, you have to move to Los Angeles. You cannot get in the film business if you don't live in L.A. You can remain in it in other cities, but you have to start here.

You need to have enough money to live for two months while you're looking for a job. There are two ways to go about finding one: through an acquaintance or through a temp agency. There are a dozen really good entertainment temp agencies, and lots of people have gotten good temp jobs that have led to permanent positions in the movie business.

Everyone knows someone in L.A. I knew only one person—who wasn't even working in the film business then—but he introduced me to a friend of his at Disney, and that's how I got my job. One person.

You can't help but notice good people. They are in your face saying, "Can I help you?" And you don't have to tell them something 15 times. Things actually get done. Don't feel like you have to move up the ladder. Just work hard. Get the job done and you will be noticed.

Minority Report (2002)   A.I. Artificial Intelligence (2001)   Saving Private Ryan (1998, coproducer)   Amistad (1997, associate producer)   The Lost World: Jurassic Park (1997, associate producer)   Schindler's List (1993, production associate)

GREAT WOMEN OF FILM   17

CHRISTINE VACHON

PRODUCER

The big myth about independent films is that they're independent. They're not. No movie is independent.
The movie is coming from somewhere, either from Sony or Miramax or Mr. Jones. Whoever is putting the money up
wants it back. Some studios are better than others, and some investors are easier than others, but I find it very facile
to say there's any difference between independent films and studio films. Not in my perception.

I STARTED WORKING IN FILM in the late 1980s as a production assistant, a second assistant director, and then as a first assistant director. It was clear to me very early on that producing was the engine of a movie. It was the role I could play: put all of the elements together and make it all happen. To me, that was the most exciting thing.

Christine Vachon's first movie was Todd Haynes's debut feature, Poison, *which won the Grand Jury Prize at the Sundance Film Festival in 1991. Since then, her New York-based company, Killer Films, has produced two to four films a year.*

People say a low-budget film is under what, $5 million? How low-budget is that? Really, when you think about it in relevance to your life, it's a lot of money. So even when you're making movies for what seems like lunch money to Hollywood, you're still throwing around a lot of money, and that's a tremendous responsibility.

I don't make charity movies. I make commercial movies, which most of the time manage to make their money back and then some; or, at worst, don't lose a tremendous amount for the people who've invested.

There's no magic formula—no one can ever think of what makes a movie work. On a panel, some idiot, whom I won't name, once said to me, "The problem with a lot of first-time filmmakers is their movies are so uncommercial, and they should, for their first film, try and make a commercial movie." And I wanted to say, "If anyone could figure that out, we'd all be fucking doing it! We'd all be in our houses in Bermuda." Nobody knows. I go into most of my films with a tremendous amount of optimism, but I couldn't have told you beforehand which ones would hit and which ones wouldn't. Sometimes I look at the dailies and go, "Man, this is incredible! This one is going to be the one!" And then it goes nowhere. And other times, I look and I go, "Oh, God! I so don't know about this one." And then it goes to the top. But again, that's what makes it fun. The only thing that makes it hard is that what you learn in the process of making one movie isn't really stuff that you could apply to the next.

WHAT I LOOK FOR IN A PROJECT

Number one, is the script original, exciting, and provocative? Am I excited about seeing it on-screen? Secondly, is the director collaborative? Can I work with him or her? Do they seem completely psychotic, or are they articulate and communicative about their ideas and vision? And thirdly, is it something I can sell? It doesn't mean that it has to be a blockbuster, but there has to be an element to it with which I can excite a potential financier, whether it's a great performance by Hilary Swank in *Boys Don't Cry,* or a wonderful concept like *Series 7.* Those are the things I look for.

A CERTAIN STAGE OF READINESS

Each movie has a different time line. *Boys Don't Cry* was in development for five years while we struggled to find financing. *One Hour Photo,* the Mark Romanek film we did with Robin Williams, took only nine months to set up at Fox Searchlight. I don't know why that happened so quickly—perhaps because the director was at a certain stage of readiness, and the script was in a certain stage of readiness. And even though it was frustrating to wait five years to get *Boys Don't Cry* made, the script just got better and better, and the director got better and better. So sometimes it's a blessing in disguise. Sometimes you sort of miss your moment, and it feels like if it doesn't get made at a certain time, it's not going to.

A GREAT PRODUCER

A great producer finds the financing and puts the elements together. She develops the script. She is at once a cheerleader, a hand-holder, and the person who is constantly trying to convince everybody else that the glass is half full even though it seems to be half empty. I think a great producer is a locomotive, keeping everything on track and keeping everything moving. Directors really need to concentrate fairly exclusively on the story and what's happening in front of the camera. A producer has to be able to see the movie in its place in the world at all times.

Movies get made a hundred million different ways. Movies get financed a hundred million different ways. A movie isn't any less of a movie because the financing came from Uncle Fred as opposed to MGM. What matters is what ends up on celluloid.

A producer has to be able to identify talent, to nurture it, take care of it, and not, in the process, mash what makes a great director, or an actor, or a great production designer special.

One of the great things about film is that it's the sum of its parts. One of the unfortunate things, especially in this country, is that film is considered a director's art, and a director's art only. Great directors make a difference, they absolutely do. But one of the things that keeps people going back again and again is the idea of working with a great team, being part of a collaborative effort. A great team can make everybody look good. A great designer makes the director of photography look fantastic, who makes the costume designer look fantastic. A composer makes everybody look great as well. That's what filmmaking is all about. I think the kind of producer that I am, and that I try to train

people to be, is one who is able to prioritize, who maintains a certain degree of calmness in the face of difficult odds, and is able to take enormous leaps of faith without losing too much sleep.

I worry a lot about wanna-be filmmakers who don't have such a strong sense of film history. The great directors I've worked with know films, and go and see other people's films all the time. They're obsessed with great moviemaking, and I think that has an impact on the movies they're making.

I can't think of any advice anybody ever gave me that really stuck to me or mattered, except "Be on time," which I think is pretty much the best advice you can give anybody.

Storytelling (2002) The Grey Zone (2001) One Hour Photo (2001) The Safety of Objects (2001) Women in Film (2001) Series 7: The Contenders (2001) Hedwig and the Angry Inch (2001) Crime and Punishment in Suburbia (2000) Boys Don't Cry (1999) I'm Losing You (1999) Velvet Goldmine (1998) Happiness (1998) Office Killer (1997) Kiss Me, Guido (1997) I Shot Andy Warhol (1996) Stonewall (1996) Kids (1995, coproducer) Safe (1995) Go Fish (1994, executive producer) Swoon (1992) Poison (1991)

JANE ROSENTHAL

PRODUCER

If you cannot trust your own instincts, you shouldn't be in this business. It's all about believing in something. That doesn't necessarily mean that every movie you believe in will be a success. David Picker once said, "If I said yes to all the movies I didn't want to do, and no to all the movies I did, I'd still have the same track record."

I WANTED TO BE AN ACTRESS, but my parents refused to put me through school if I majored in acting. So I majored in film and television at NYU, thinking I would then be able to act in student films. But I quickly discovered acting was not for me because my fate was out of my control. While I liked the process of acting, I didn't like the fact that anyone could just dismiss me.

At 18, Jane Rosenthal produced a workshop at the Actors Studio in New York with Pete Masterson, who cowrote, with Larry L. King, The Best Little Whorehouse in Texas. *She went with the show first to Off Broadway, and then to Broadway, as Masterson's assistant. She also worked for CBS, first on a soap opera, then as a researcher for* The NFL Today. *Moving to Los Angeles, she worked in the network's miniseries and movies-of-the-week department. "It wasn't until after I'd done miniseries for a year, and over 70 television movies in five years on every subject matter, social issue, disease of the week … I needed to do something else," she recalls. After that, Rosenthal gravitated to feature films.*

I spent two and a half years at Disney with Michael Eisner and Jeffrey Katzenberg. I learned an incredible skill set from them. But once I got to the level of vice president, I didn't want to do it, because it was not about making movies, it was about the business of making movies. It didn't interest me as much.

I was working with Martin Scorsese at the time, as his executive on *The Color of Money.* Watching his process was fascinating. Marty probably gave me my biggest career break, one that radically changed my life. He told me his friend Bob De Niro was starting a movie company in New York, and would I be interested in talking to him? I met De Niro, and we talked on and off for a good nine months. My lawyer and my various advisors all said, "You must be crazy. The movie business is in Los Angeles, not in New York. You are committing career suicide." But when I talked to Bob, I felt I had to try something new.

I remember going away to a place in the desert for the weekend. I'm not a person who makes lists, but I wrote a list of pros, cons, and intangibles. When I got done, the pros outweighed the cons,

and the intangibles were basically going to be the intangibles my whole life. I thought if I couldn't trust my own instinct and move to New York and try this, I should give up the business anyway. I had no family responsibilities at that time. I could sell my car, rent out my house.

Rosenthal was 30 when she started the Tribeca Film Center with Robert De Niro.

I moved into this little apartment and worked with Bob on purchasing the film center. I just kept blinders on in terms of what other people were saying. There were days when I cried, not because I was having second thoughts, but because I was so lonely. We spent time sitting there talking about what we would call this company. I suggested Tribeca because when my friends in L.A. would ask where I was living, I responded, "Tribeca." They said, "But we thought you moved to New York!" To them it sounded like I was in New Jersey. Once we renovated the building, a hundred-year-old former coffee plant, it felt like we had a real place. After our first movie, *Thunderheart,* went into production, I felt like, "Okay, we're doing it."

I wanted one of our early movies to be something Bob didn't star in, so people would understand the company wasn't going to just make quirky macho pictures, which is what he was then known for doing. I also looked for projects he could direct. After *Thunderheart* came *Night and the City,* which Irwin Winkler directed and Bob was in, and *A Bronx Tale,* which Bob starred in with Chazz Palminteri and directed.

FINDING A PROJECT YOU CAN MARRY

I try to find good stories I can feel passionate about, because a movie takes so long to get off the ground that it becomes a marriage. You need to nurture it and guide it through sickness and health, till death do you part. I have to be able to relate to the stories I choose on some emotional level. I could never make a science-fiction movie because I'm not into it. And I just don't get movies that have a certain blatant violence.

You get to see the downside of this business when the movie you have believed in flops. For me it was *The Adventures of Rocky and Bullwinkle.* I worked so hard for so many years to get it made. It bombed—and with such a thud it was heartwrenching. That was very, very painful.

I honestly did walk around feeling as if somebody had died. It didn't work, that's the bottom line. I learned more from that than from my successes. It keeps you humble, and it roots you back in reality.

There's a lot more collaboration with a studio that's spending $100 million on a movie—no one has a singular voice. If you're spending $8 million, then there can be more of an auteur on the picture. I do most of our films with major studios. Sometimes you have to fight for the talent you believe will bring the role to life. It's not just like, "This actor would be amazing in this role." The studio may want the newest young actor, or somebody with a proven track record.

In terms of production, some advances are really exciting. Digital editing has already changed the economics of the movie business. Before a film is wrapped, I can see the whole thing cut together, because the director and editor work on an Avid. It's faster and more cost-efficient.

When gearing up for production, I'm working with the writer and the director, collaborating on hiring all the essential personnel. My day-to-day responsibility is the movie, in which case I'm on set every day. You have this incredible, creative group of people who are all there together, everyone with their insane egos. If you can get the production to run like an incredibly well-oiled machine, and it goes out and does what it's supposed to do, then I know I've done a good job. No one is supposed to notice producing, it should happen seamlessly.

When it comes to hiring, usually it's a gut instinct. I like smart people who have good ideas and are not afraid of their own opinions. We hire a lot of people right out of school, and even those who are still in school. You get a certain knowledge base from film school, although film school isn't absolutely necessary. Just have a well-rounded education and be an avid reader. It's good to know movie history and to watch movies, but you should also have a strong background in literature and history. Because, at the end of the day, it goes back to good stories. That's what people want: stories they can relate to.

About a Boy (2002)   Showtime (2002)   Meet the Parents (2000)   The Adventures of Rocky and Bullwinkle (2000)   Flawless (1999)   Entropy (1999)   Analyze This (1999)
Wag the Dog (1997)   Marvin's Room (1996)   Faithful (1996)   Panther (1995)   The Night We Never Met (1993)   A Bronx Tale (1993)   Night and the City (1992)
Thunderheart (1992)   Mistress (1992)

If you use the imagery of climbing the ladder, it's infinity. There's always something else you have to strive for. It's not so much a ladder, but learning curves that take you through your career.

KASI LEMMONS

WRITER/DIRECTOR

*With both of the movies I directed, there were so many times that if the word "no" actually meant "no" to me,
I never would've done them. The ability to hear "no" a hundred, two hundred times, and still not give up—that's hard.
Somehow you have to wake up with the same hopes and dreams every day and not let them get squashed.*

WHEN I WAS NINE YEARS OLD, my mother put me into Boston Children's Theatre. My parents had just gotten divorced, and I think she wanted me to be cheerful and occupied. I knew then that I wanted to be an artist, an actor, or something like that.

I moved to New York, started off doing commercials, and then some theater. The first film I did was Spike Lee's *School Daze.* Then I went to film school at the New School for Social Research. *The Silence of the Lambs* was my big break as an actor, and shortly after that I wrote *Eve's Bayou.*

I had always been writing, since I was a little kid. In film school I started writing scenes for friends to do in acting class—little two-person scenes with no context. I got kind of famous for it. Acting teachers started to ask, "Who wrote that?" That was how I got started. And then a man broke my heart, and I wrote a play about it. That was my first full-length play.

In my twenties I realized that if I were going to be an actress, as an African American woman I was going to have a lot of free time on my hands. And I wasn't too keen on that. I had a lot of creative energy, and I wasn't using it. I thought I was going to make documentaries, do something important for humanity—go to Nicaragua with the camera, make social statements.

Some of my early influences may seem a bit warped or weird, but I'm really attracted to looking at perspectives that are askew. I remember when I first saw *Rosemary's Baby,* I thought, "Wow, that's powerful!" You could be scary and funny and profound at the same time. I thought the idea of an actor selling his firstborn child to the devil for a part was really cool.

Eve's Bayou was a story I had in my head, my big American epic. I could tell you the story way before I ever wrote anything down. It was something that I felt very close to. I stopped acting after writing *Eve's*

Bayou and became a writer, which I never would have foreseen. *Eve's Bayou* was a question I needed to get off my chest—although it could not be answered. It had to do with the nature of reality: Is a subjective point of view all there is, or is there such a thing as an objective reality that can be measured? If two people go through the same experience, and remember it in two completely different ways, which is the truth? That question fascinated me, and that's what *Eve's Bayou* is all about.

I was flattered and encouraged when people understood what I wanted to say, because I thought it was one of my kinks, and I really didn't know if anybody would respond to it. It was a life-affirming experience, and it gave me faith in the power of art to communicate.

I think it's important for first-time filmmakers to say something completely personal.
The best way to go into your first writing experience is with something that you've written purely for yourself that reflects you and the questions on your mind.

THE CREW CAN MAKE YOU OR BREAK YOU

Working with people is the most exciting part of filmmaking for me. I think it's a mistake to underestimate the importance of any crew member. A job as simple as craft services can make your day if they come in at just the right time, with just the right snack that wakes the crew up. It's the human effort that makes a film.

A very wise man once said to me, "You never want to get to the point where you don't want to get out of bed. You want to wake up each day and say, Okay, it's a new day! We're going to shoot and it's gonna be great!" You really do begin to run on a kind of adrenaline energy that is manufactured inside of you because nobody is meant to work 80 hours a week. The challenging part about is that as a director, you should be able to bring everybody in the crew with you on this ride.

Writer: Eve's Bayou (1997) Dr. Hugo (1996, short) Director: The Caveman's Valentine (2001) Eve's Bayou (1997) Dr. Hugo (1996, short) Actor: Liars' Dice (1998)
'Til There Was You (1997) Gridlock'd (1997) Drop Squad (1994) Fear of a Black Hat (1994) Hard Target (1993) Candyman (1992) The Five Heartbeats (1991)
The Silence of the Lambs (1991) Vampire's Kiss (1989) School Daze (1988)

ALLISON ANDERS
WRITER/DIRECTOR/MOM

I always have the same experience with making movies: it's pure heaven and pure hell at the same time. Wim Wenders once told me that the production always reflects what the film is about. Every time, I find this is true. That's why you'd better be careful what you decide to make your movies about.

I DROPPED OUT OF HIGH SCHOOL, and I went back to junior college when my first baby was born. When my second baby was born, I had to stay home with her, so I wrote a book about teen movies. It didn't get published, but it sparked my interest in movies.

When I saw Wim Wenders's films, I thought, "That's what I want to do." This is an incredible story, but I started loading him down with fan mail. I wrote him my first fan letter and sent it to his agent. When he didn't write back after a whole week, I called his agent. They said my letter had been sent to his home in New York City. So I checked with Information, and he was listed in the phone book.

I called him up, and he was just hanging out watching football on TV. I go, "Hi, are you Wim Wenders, the director?" (As if there would be two in the world.) "I'm Allison Anders, and I sent you a letter." He was like, "Oh yeah, the big one," because my letter was ten pages long. I had also sent him a tape of an all-girl band, because he had such cool music in his films. He said, "I really like the tape you sent me, but I don't write letters very much. If you want to keep writing to me, you can." Boy, he had just opened Pandora's box! And so I sent him these letters, huge letters—one was like 60 pages long. People were like, "What do you write to this guy?" I said, "I don't know, things that I'm thinking about, my children, myself, bands that I've seen."

It took me two years to get into UCLA. When I got accepted, he sent me a congratulations postcard. When I was making my first film at UCLA, he called me and said, "Allison, this is Wim. I wonder if you could find time to show me your film?" He came to UCLA and saw my movie. You can imagine I was just stunned.

Because I was a single mom on welfare, I was very good at scamming, so I lied my ass off to get a film grant. I said I needed it because Wim Wenders had invited me to study under him on *Paris, Texas.* Then I said to Wim, "Look, I won this grant. It's actually to study under you on *Paris,*

Texas." He just looked up at the ceiling with this faraway look and said, "Well, I guess you have to come."

On *Paris, Texas,* I learned from him as much as I possibly could. And he still has all of my letters, filed away. I'm sure they are very embarrassing.

I had gotten into UCLA with Kurt Voss, my very close friend and writing partner. We wanted to make a feature, and thought, "We've got $2,000, so let's do it." Dean Lent shot the movie, and the three of us were the crew. We approached all of these post-punk, local rock stars to be in the movie, and wrote the script around them. This helped us complete the movie because we got local press and we got a soundtrack deal. The movie was called *Border Radio.*

ESCAPING TO A FANTASY WORLD

I actually learned my craft well before I got into school. It started as a survival instinct, and ended up being my job.

When I was 15 years old, I put together a whole fantasy world for myself because my home life was not so good. I went a little bit off the deep end. It was 1969, and there were rumors that Paul McCartney was dead, and all of these clues on the album cover and stuff. To escape my home life, I got really into it. I started to believe that I was actually communicating through a Ouija board with a dead Paul McCartney. This actually saved my life, because it transported me into this fantasy world where I learned to create characters, talk to them, and make up stories. Of course, it landed me in a couple of mental hospitals, but it was better than where I was living.

I had a psychosomatic pregnancy, and when people would ask me who the father was, I would say Paul McCartney—only the dead one. Eventually, my pregnancy disappeared, and I went hitchhiking across the country. Paul finally confessed that he wasn't really Paul McCartney, but just a regular dead guy. I thought, "Well, it's been nice knowing you. If you're not the Beatle, there are plenty of cute, live guys out here." When I look back, that's the beginning of my career as a filmmaker.

GRACE OF MY HEART

The most difficult movie I've made was *Grace of My Heart*. It was the most ambitious. It was the most involved. And all of the little details in the clothes and the production design, the music—all stuff done by my amazing crew—I'm still in love with when I see the movie. I thought, "My God, look at these extras! They look so good, so real. Look at these locations, look at these sets, and the music, it's exquisite." I'm very, very proud of the team we had.

I got the idea for *Mi Vida Loca* when I was living in the Echo Park neighborhood of Los Angeles. I'd see the Latina girls walking down the street, and they just fascinated me. I learned very quickly that this was not my neighborhood, but that I was living in their neighborhood.

I didn't necessarily know their culture, but I knew their class. I'd been raised poor, and as a teenage mom I had dealt with food stamps. That was the thing that bonded me to the girls.

I met one of the girls, the youngest one. I kind of hit her up because she seemed like she wasn't going to kick my ass. I told her—Whisper, who plays Whisper in the movie—that I wanted to write something about the girls of Echo Park. She eventually set it up. I also had to get the help of the local drug dealer, who was a drug dealer turned probation officer.

The girls gave me this really cool slang dictionary. It has black street slang and Latino street slang. That was enormously helpful. I would ask them, "Do you still use this word? Is this word kind of out now?" They'd go through and tell me different slang words; some are Spanish and some are Spanglish.

When I look at my movies now, I know I made a lot of mistakes. But to me, mistakes are interesting as well. I would hope critics would allow filmmakers to make mistakes, understanding that it's all part of the process; I learned things on *Four Rooms* that were invaluable to me in making my next movie.

NO PLACE FOR BIG EGOS

As for my crew, I try to stay away from people with ego problems. I don't want that on my set, even if I work with big stars. I like to work with real actors, not people who are trying to be celebrities.

As a director, I give a lot of freedom to my crew. I'm very specific and give them a lot of information so that I can trust them to know what kind of wardrobe, sets, props, and makeup they should come up with.

I really do believe that directing actors happens primarily through casting and communication. Basically, my job is to create an atmosphere of safety for the actors. And safety is individual. Some actors need lots of freedom; others need none because they don't feel safe unless you tell them exactly what to do.

I don't like very many movie scores. I think they sound too bombastic and phony. My composers are often rock musicians, usually doing their first score. On *Border Radio,* Dave Alvin did an amazing score with our tiny budget. J Mascis did my score with Dinosaur Jr for *Gas Food Lodging.* For *Mi Vida Loca,* I got John Taylor of Duran Duran. And Sonic Youth did *Things Behind the Sun.*

THE ROUTE TO DIRECTING

My advice to a young girl who wants to become a director? Fall absolutely madly in love with anybody. If it's the wrong person, all the better, then you'll have something to make a movie about. Pay attention to subcultures in your town—there are those in every town. Make a movie about what you know. Pay attention to how people talk—in your family, in your town. Really pay attention to little details of character. And watch as many movies as possible, preferably the old ones on TCM and AMC—even the silent movies, because they have many good, solid story ideas.

Listen to a lot of music, which always stimulates creativity. Try to get into film school, because film theory is important. You need to know that you didn't invent the dolly move, and that it was invented for a reason (probably by a woman, but D.W. Griffith got credit for it, right?).

If you cannot get into film school, hook up with other filmmakers, either through Independent Feature Project or Sundance. IFP has a great program called "Project Involve" for young women. You can get to the IFP from anywhere in the country.

Allison Anders started Women Filmmakers Summit, which evolved into a group called 50/50.

I started 50/50 because I discovered that, to my surprise, there were all these women film directors in the early history of motion pictures whom I knew nothing about. That was really shocking and sad to me, and I felt robbed. It's amazing—women didn't have the right to vote in this country, but they had successful careers as film directors.

FORGOTTEN WOMEN OF EARLY HOLLYWOOD

Women of early Hollywood were responsible for many inventions. Dorothy Arzner invented the boom mike. She had the sound guy stick the microphone on a fishing rod so that her actors could move around the room, instead of having to step up to a mike in the middle of the room. Lois Weber was the highest-paid director during her time,

earning more than any of the men. And Dorothy Arzner beat every one at the box office. Part of our goal is to make sure that women won't again be forgotten.

It was very intense for me to be working on what used to be the MGM lot—now the Sony lot—where Dorothy Arzner made her movies. I saw no trace of her anywhere, but instead big monuments and billboards named after every guy who had systematically gotten rid of her and every other woman director of the past. Once someone realized, "Hey, we can make a lot of money in this industry," they got rid of the women and the minorities. The discrimination wasn't necessarily expressed in words, but slowly, over the years, women were not directing movies anymore.

DIGITAL FILMMAKING REVOLUTION

The girl who is starting out today has one advantage over those in years past: she can afford to buy herself a digital camera.

I think that in a couple of years, young women will arrive with their digital cameras and their fuck-you attitudes and take the riot-grrrl thing to a whole new filmic level. Digital filmmaking is great for women because it's not a borrowed medium. Even though we helped create the film, it was taken away from us so early that it feels borrowed. We can really possess digital filmmaking in a way that we could never possess film, because we got axed out too early.

Things Behind the Sun (2001, TV) Grosse Pointe (2000, TV) Sex and the City (1999–2000, TV) Sugar Town (1999) Grace of My Heart (1996) Four Rooms (1995, "The Missing Ingredient" segment) Mi Vida Loca (1993) Gas Food Lodging (1992) Border Radio (1987)

JANE ANDERSON

DIRECTOR/WRITER

Directing is enormously stressful. The most important thing is to maintain your stamina.
You need good shoes, and you need to eat well. You need to sleep, because once you start production, you're
working 16-hour days. It is truly like leading an army. That's why I like it. I like being a general.

WHEN I WAS 19, I dropped out of college and went straight to New York City because I wanted to be an actress. That was the best thing I could have done, because I was exposed to all forms of humanity, different class and racial structures, bag ladies, crazy people. Everywhere I went there was a wonderful piece of drama going on. I learned how to write dialogue by keeping my ears open when riding on the subway and walking down the street.

My initial break was in David Mamet's first New York hit, a little Off-Broadway show called *Sexual Perversity in Chicago.* I learned how to say dirty words on stage. Acting in this play also taught me how to write, since David's writing is very sparse and very lean, and his dialogue is very true.

I became a comedian, and came to Los Angeles with a show. It folded, but I stayed and got some writing gigs on a couple of TV shows.

Then the space shuttle Challenger blew up, and I wrote my first play, *Defying Gravity.* I was so deeply shaken by the event that I had to write about it. Being a playwright made me very popular in Hollywood because producers would much rather hire a playwright to ruin their work than hire a television writer to ruin their work—I guess there's farther to go. Then I started writing screenplays along with plays.

After two of my screenplays were made into major movies, I knew I wanted to direct. I had gotten an Emmy for *The Positively True Adventures of the Alleged Texas Cheerleader-Murdering Mom.* And, although I had gained respect as a writer, I didn't think anybody would give me the opportunity to direct.

One of my plays, *The Baby Dance,* went to New York after a long regional run, and critic Frank Rich made sure it would never play there again. I thought the whole thing was dead. Then a producer suggested that I could direct the movie. We went to Jodie Foster, and she decided to take a chance on me and produce the film. It's a very big deal to mentor a first-time director; you don't know if they're going to totally blow it and ruin your reputation. She gave me a lot of creative freedom and advice when I needed it.

We all need that in our careers. Somebody in the business who believes in you, and who is powerful enough to give you your first chance.

A MOVIE IS ULTIMATELY THE DIRECTOR'S VISION

A screenwriter has to make peace with the fact that once she turns her script in and does her revisions, she's going to have very little control over what happens to the script. That's the nature of the business. It is ultimately the director's vision, because the director creates the visual elements, directs the actors, chooses the music, and, most importantly, edits the film, which is another form of rewriting.

I think every writer and director should take an acting class. Be on stage, get in front of the camera, and learn what it's like to be really vulnerable. One thing Jodie taught me when I was about to direct, she said: "Just remember, as tired as you are by the end of the day, the actor will be even more tired." I think it's true—except the actor gets to go home or to the trailer, while the director is on to the next horrible problem to be solved. And if you're writing as well as directing, you'll be working on the script all weekend while everybody else is sleeping.

 <u>Director:</u> When Billie Beat Bobby (2001, TV) If These Walls Could Talk 2 (2000, TV, segment "1961") The Baby Dance (1998, TV) <u>Writer:</u> When Billie Beat Bobby (2001, TV) If These Walls Could Talk 2 (2000, TV, segment "1961") The Baby Dance (1998, TV) How to Make an American Quilt (1995) It Could Happen to You (1994) The Positively True Adventures of the Alleged Texas Cheerleader-Murdering Mom (1993, TV) <u>Playwright:</u> Looking for Normal Defying Gravity The Baby Dance Food and Shelter The Last Time We Saw Her Lynette at 3 a.m. Tough Choices for the New Century

A Day in the Life of a Director

5:00 a.m. Alarm goes off for 6 a.m. call. Creep out of bed without waking spouse. Shower and slip on clothes that I have preset the night before.

5:30 a.m. Assistant is at door to pick me up (don't trust my own driving during a shoot). Kiss sleeping spouse and son goodbye. While driving to the set, go over the day's pages. Pray that I'll make it.

6:00 a.m. Arrive at the set. Try to look cheerful, confident, and awake. Grab breakfast from the truck and take in nourishment while answering questions from first assistant director (can you lose at least three setups?); second assistant director (where do you want the extras?); prop master (which of these ten umbrellas do you prefer?); costume designer (do you want so-and-so to wear a leather jacket or a sweater vest?); production designer (can you look at the floor plan for next week's set?).

6:15 a.m. Visit the makeup trailer: approve wigs, teeth, scars, tan lines, etc. Go over line changes with actors.

en to their concerns about the day's scenes. Do a quick
write if necessary. Instill confidence when necessary.

0 a.m. Join the director of photography on the set.
cuss the first setup, which has been carefully planned
weeks before, but will now completely change after
t to the makeup trailer. Actors come on the set to
earse. Appear cheerful, confident, and in command
ile working out brand-new blocking with the producers,
istant director, stand-ins, and crew looking on and
cking their watches.

0 a.m. Actors go off to finish their hair and makeup.
ector of photography and the camera crew set up the
ts. Answer questions from the set dresser. Answer ques-
ns from the sound operator. Check the shot. Avoid the
ducer, who's still eyeing his watch.

5 a.m. Actors are back. It's time to shoot. One more
earsal. Give actors adjustments. Ask for quiet. Camera-
rson says she is ready. Say "Action." Say "Cut." And try
remember every last technical, visual, audio, and

emotional detail that went between those two words, and
determine whether it satisfies the requirements of the vision
of your film. Then ask your script supervisor what he or she
thought. Chances are the continuity was off. Make adjustments. Repeat until satisfied and the cameraperson says
that the gate is clear.

1:00 p.m. Meal break. Pee. Answer questions. Take food to
trailer and look at yesterday's dailies.

2:00 p.m. Back on the set. Shoot.

8:00 p.m. Finish last scene of the day. Say goodnight to
cast and crew. Thank everyone for a fine day of work.
Discuss tomorrow's first setup with D.P. Strategize with A.D.
Listen to long list of concerns from producer.

9:00 p.m. Drive home.

10:00 p.m. Have barely coherent conversation with spouse.
Kiss sleeping child good night. Go to bed. Shut eyes. Go
over the next day's scenes in my head. Pray that I'll make it.

2:00 a.m. Fall asleep.

VICKY JENSON, LORNA COOK, BRENDA CHAPMAN

ANIMATION DIRECTORS

Certain arts come with experience, and directing and storytelling are two of those things.
You're representing slices of life, stuff that's universal, and the only way to be able to do that is if you have
experienced something. You need to make a statement people can connect to. —Vicky Jenson

LORNA COOK: I've been drawing since I was a kid. I grew up in Burbank, in the shadow of the Disney Studios. This sounds so typical, but when I was around 19, I was watching *Lady and the Tramp,* and I had this epiphany that I wanted to do animation. I submitted a portfolio to Disney and got in on a training program in 1973, when there were very few women. I was fortunate to have Eric Larson, one of Disney's famous Nine Old Men, pioneers of animation, as my mentor.

Lorna Cook, like Brenda Chapman and Vicky Jenson, is an animation director at DreamWorks. She worked as an animator in TV and on features at Disney, and she spent 11 years at Don Bluth's animation company.

LORNA COOK: I switched gears in my profession and became a story artist because that afforded me more opportunity to mini-direct. Brenda Chapman was my dear friend and mentor in that regard, because I worked on *The Lion King* with her. At DreamWorks, I was cohead of story for *The Prince of Egypt* and then codirector on *Spirit.* I'm 51. It's been a long journey, but it's been driven by the desire to make wonderful entertainment and tell stories that inspire people.

Brenda Chapman's first film for Disney was The Little Mermaid. *She also worked on* Beauty and the Beast, *and then as head of story on* The Lion King.

BRENDA CHAPMAN: I've been drawing ever since I could hold a pencil. My mom got rid of an old coffee table once, and as she was taking it out the door she noticed all my drawings underneath. I decided to become an animator after seeing *The Secret of NIMH.* A friend of a cousin of a friend of so-and-so worked at Disney, so I got a phone number and contacted the animation studios. They directed me to Cal Arts, a school in Valencia, California, that has a character-animation program. After Cal Arts, Disney hired me as a story trainee.

Vicky Jenson worked as an art director with Ralph Bakshi and John Kricfalusi, for whom she also did development work. She was one of three art directors on FernGully. *Starting at DreamWorks in 1996, she was a production designer and story artist for* The Road to El Dorado. *She made her directorial debut with* Shrek.

VICKY JENSON: My sister and brother-in-law had their own animation company, and I was painting cels and babysitting at the same time, making a whopping five dollars an hour. After a few years I started cel-painting for some studios across from Hanna-Barbera. I was painting Smurf backgrounds and Flintstone backgrounds during the summer, partly to fund college. Little by little, it turned into a career. I ended up doing background designs and storyboards for one of the television studios. I realized I had the job a lot of my friends were trying to get.

The animation director is the highest rung on the creative ladder, and she is surrounded by a tight group of key creative personnel, including the head of story, art director, writers, and story artists.

BRENDA CHAPMAN: The director gives a general feel of what he or she is looking for in a scene. The head of story helps the story artists achieve that goal. They're free to give ideas, and we incorporate those, but the director's job is to keep a single vision while all these other incredibly creative people are bringing a lot to the table. You have to focus it all into what the film needs to be. Story is a great training ground for having a global view of the film. It's a very collaborative process.

LORNA COOK: The head of story works so closely with the director, they really are shaping the story together.

VICKY JENSON: The story artist is the first to visualize the script. You get script pages, and you start deciding when it's a close-up or a long shot.

BRENDA CHAPMAN: You're also helping the director keep the story in his or her head, because the director has all these other things to worry about. You count on your head of story to go, "Okay, you're going off track; remember, this is happening over here."

VICKY JENSON: Oftentimes we have brainstorming sessions where our writers and story artists, directors, and producers will be in the same place, hammering out ideas or throwing drawings up on the wall, trying to solve a particular problem.

LORNA COOK: Working with a codirector is like an arranged marriage, because two people never see things the same way. But if you respect each other's strengths, and allow that to be your guiding force, then you turn it into your strength. When it works, it works great, because you have someone to lean on when you're exhausted, and vice versa.

IT STARTS WITH A GREAT IDEA

BRENDA CHAPMAN: How a project gets greenlighted varies with every picture. Sometimes you'll have this great idea, and Jeffrey [Katzenberg] will go, "We're making that movie." He'll get writers and story artists to go away in a room and come up with something. Or an idea will be passed around to writers, and someone will come in with a great first-draft script.

LORNA COOK: There is no formula. *Spirit* was a beautiful novella, but once we dug deep and found the main points of the story, we realized the story was actually being developed within our group of story artists. It was a very organic process because we developed sequences on the storyboards.

VICKY JENSON: It's such a visual medium that everything has to be created. The script really becomes a kind of spine or a story core, giving you the skeleton of what each scene is about. The board artists can explore other ideas, still telling the same story we need in a sequence, but playing with the dialogue, the action, and how we introduce things. Sometimes you end up with 12 little movies in a row and work with that.

LORNA COOK: These story sketches are the blueprint of the film. Because the sophistication level has risen in the last few years using the Avid, we're making these movies in a much more complete fashion, so a lot of times it requires more drawings to say what we want to say.

VICKY JENSON: One of the benefits of animation is we get to do the movie over and over again. You pre-edit the movie. That way, when we shoot an entire story reel, we get the chance to see how it feels, how the music's working, how people are reacting to it—making adjustments before we move into the really expensive part.

TECHNOLOGY IN THE SERVICE OF STORYTELLING

VICKY JENSON: Story drives everything. Technology doesn't drive a story. In *Shrek*, there were a lot of things we knew we needed to do, but the technology wasn't there yet. We just had to have faith it would get there. We didn't know how to do fire. We

weren't sure how we were going to do beer mixing with mud. Milk needed to look like milk. You don't want people looking at it and going, "Oh, how cool, that's CG (computer-generated) milk!" You just want them to forget about the technology and sink into the story.

Some of what we did in *Shrek* was very much like live action. We had sort of virtual cameras set up in the computer. You could move through a set and pick out lenses, block out action with stand-in characters that could do a bit of rudimentary animation, so the layout artists could be like a cinematographer. Instead of having to draw a close-up, like when you have a two-shot in 2-D and you have to draw one guy bigger and one guy smaller, here we could actually choose: Is it a long lens, or does one character move toward the camera, or does the camera move toward him?

FOR ADULTS AS WELL AS CHILDREN

BRENDA CHAPMAN: It's hard to accept that the industry views us as stepchildren. A lot of blood, sweat, and tears go into creating these things, and people have committed their lives to this career—not just for making kiddie fare, but stories that touch people all over the world.

VICKY JENSON: *Aladdin* broke a lot of ground when it came to introducing more adult humor. I think cultural references made it really different. That movie came alive once the genie showed up. You don't have to talk down to kids anymore; they're capable of understanding a lot. Kids can grow into the other aspects of a movie, as long as you're not trying to talk over their heads too much.

BRENDA CHAPMAN: That's the great thing about the old Bugs Bunny cartoons. It's adult humor, but kids love that stuff.

OBSERVE LIFE AND DRAW EVERYTHING YOU SEE

BRENDA CHAPMAN: Aiming for a story position is best, but sometimes the work isn't up to par when you're fresh out of school. If you can't find any training positions or internships in story, try to get a job in the clean-up department, where they will teach you to be a great draftsman. While you're honing your skills there, start talking to people in the department you want to focus on.

The women recommend such schools as Cal Arts in Valencia, the Academy of Arts in San Francisco, and the Ringling School of Art in Florida. (These schools are also listed in the Appendix.) But, Jenson notes, "That first job is so important. Most of what I learned was on the job."

LORNA COOK: Find mentors who can really help you. Spend a lot of time looking over their shoulders, asking questions, tailing them if allowed. Be a student of film, but watch life and humanity. See how people really think and feel and talk. Draw your butt off, become very good at your skill level, and build it all the time. Travel. Have adventures!

VICKY JENSON: Pick up filmmaking books. There's a cinematography book called *Shot by Shot*, which is like Storyboarding 101. Draw comics. If you see something funny, draw it, and write some dialogue.

 <u>Vicky Jenson:</u> Shrek (2001, codirector) The Road to El Dorado (2000, production design/story artist) FernGully: The Last Rainforest (1992, art director) The Baby Huey Show (1991, TV, coproducer) Beethoven (1991, TV, art director) The Ren & Stimpy Show (1991, TV) Playroom (1990, production designer) She's Having a Baby (1988, storyboard) Slamdance (1987, storyboard) <u>Lorna Cook:</u> Spirit: Stallion of Cimarron (2002, codirector) The Prince of Egypt (1998, costory supervisor) Mulan (1998, story artist) The Lion King (1994, story artist/animator) Beauty and the Beast (1991, animator) The Secret of NIMH (1982, animator) All Dogs Go to Heaven (1989, directing animator) The Land Before Time (1988, directing animator) An American Tail (1986, animator) Pete's Dragon (1977, animator) <u>Brenda Chapman:</u> The Prince of Egypt (1998, codirector) The Hunchback of Notre Dame (1996, story artist) The Lion King (1994, head of story) Beauty and the Beast (1991, story artist) The Rescuers Down Under (1990, story artist) The Little Mermaid (1989, story artist)

FREIDA LEE MOCK

DOCUMENTARY FILMMAKER

To me, documentary films are not any different from fiction films. Both can tell powerful,
amazing stories that say something about the human spirit and the human condition.

I STUDIED HISTORY AND LAW AT UC BERKELEY with no interest in film or any of the media arts. After I had been out of college for a couple of years, teaching high school economics and history, the idea just hit me: I'm going to make documentary films.

My idea behind it was terribly arrogant—I wanted to teach people. I wanted to convey ideas about politics and social justice. Luckily, I happened to be in Los Angeles, the best place to start if you didn't go to film school. I told a friend I was interested in documentary films, and she put me in touch with David Wolper Productions, which made *National Geographic* series and Jacques Cousteau documentaries. They happened to have an opening in the research department, which was the way women usually got started in those days. At that time, most documentaries were shown only on television, whereas today you see a lot more of them playing in theaters and art houses.

In the early '80s, Freida Lee Mock launched Sanders & Mock Productions with her husband, Terry Sanders. They also cofounded the American Film Foundation to produce films on the arts, sciences, and humanities. Among their early Oscar-nominated works were the documentary shorts To Live or Let Die *(1982), examining the ethical dilemmas of caring for damaged newborns, and* Rose Kennedy: A Life to Remember *(1990).*

When we began, about half the projects were supported by grants. Basically, I did everything from making coffee to writing proposals to directing and producing. By writing grant proposals, I quickly learned where the money sources were. Nowadays, government funding has almost totally dried up. There's a lot less money available, and the competition is probably greater than ever.

Mock wrote, directed, and produced Maya Lin: A Strong Clear Vision, *which won an Academy Award for Best Feature Documentary in 1994.*

The film on Maya Lin was a total leap of faith. There was nothing but a blank piece of paper and my desire to make a film. She designed the Vietnam Veterans Memorial in Washington, D.C., and when I heard she was about to design her second and last monument—the Civil Rights Memorial—I thought it was a great opportunity to do a portrait film about the creative process, focusing on this artist grappling with these two big ideas, war and race.

The critical thing about starting an independent film project, whether fiction or nonfiction, is you have to have a strong leap of faith that it will happen. Where that comes from, I'm not sure. But I really knew that *Maya Lin* would be made. When you have that conviction, it helps you focus, especially on the funding. I was lucky to receive an initial grant of $10,000, but it took five years to raise the money, all the way to the end when I was getting the film out of the lab. In situations like this, you kind of trade off, asking people to work for less or deferring payments. While I was doing *Maya Lin*, I had other commissioned projects that helped me survive.

WHEN A STORY IS STARING YOU IN THE FACE

After *Maya Lin*, I said I would never self-start another film. But a couple of years later, at a writer's conference in Idaho, I heard the closing address by novelist and humorist Anne Lamott. I knew nothing about her; I just saw this funny title called *Bird by Bird*, which I later learned was a best-selling book. She was the funniest person I had ever heard speak, but she was also serious and deep. I thought she would be a great subject. She could sustain a film as a portrait, and she also had an interesting story. She could talk not only about writing but also about life.

So I went up to her afterward and said, "I'd like to make a film on you." I wrote her a brief letter and sent her some of my films, and she said yes. I followed her for over a year and a half. Luckily, she was coming out with a new book, so there were things to film other than a writer sitting there for eight hours. I wasn't looking for a story, but when it's staring you in the face, you go with it.

In addition to directing the Lamott film, Bird by Bird with Annie, *Mock wrote, directed, and produced, together with Terry Sanders, the theatrical feature documentary* Return with Honor, *about American pilot POWs held in North Vietnam.*

Return with Honor was done relatively fast, within a year's time. It was a very big film, almost two hours. We were filming all over the United States and Vietnam. The relationship with our backers was fabulous. They trusted me, my project, and the whole team. They were not filmmakers; they were CEOs and very smart finance people who had also been involved with the war.

Just like fiction, documentaries depend on great characters that captivate the audience. In the case of *Return with Honor*, it all depended on how a given pilot came across to us. As long as someone was spontaneous, I could tell he would be interesting. I think I interviewed 25 pilots, and 21 made it into the film. It wasn't difficult to get wonderful things from them because they were extremely articulate and candid.

Casting is important with every movie, and documentaries are no exception. You have to cast people whom the audience wants to sympathize with. I just finished a film on a children's chorus. There were 200 singers, but I could focus on only three or four to tell that composite story. You quickly find the ones that have that special something that draws the camera to them. I trust my instincts about whether a certain person is going to work.

PORTRAY THE HUMAN SPIRIT

The stock-in-trade of documentary filmmaking is to be unobtrusive. I don't like to come with ten or twenty people and lots of lights. That alters the scene. My basic crew might be the cinematographer, the camera assistant, the sound person, maybe a gaffer, plus the director/producer and the writer, who is usually one and the same person.

The most important thing is building a sense of trust with your subjects. Once you have their trust, they will allow you into their lives. I'm amazed at the candor and the lack of self-censorship, and the things that come up in an interview. People want to spill, not confessionally, but tell you what is really on their minds.

To find the truth of whatever story I'm trying to tell, I have to remember that it's not my story. If I have an agenda, that's going to alter the story. And if it involves something that the person would never want exposed to an audience of millions, I feel a great responsibility to not put that into a film.

Responsibility is a central issue for a documentarian. I prefer not to exploit people, because the relationship is already potentially exploitative. You don't want to make them look foolish or show stuff that doesn't serve the story. Another much-debated question is, If you are covering war as a documentary filmmaker, do you pick up a camera or a Band-Aid when somebody gets hurt? I think if I could save a life, I'd throw the camera away and save a life. You should also ask yourself, "Do I really need that grisly stuff? Can I show it more creatively?" Not that you don't want attention, but you need to respect your audience's intelligence.

ARE YOU STILL WORKING ON THAT?

Two years is a pretty typical time line for an independent film, unless an angel pops up and gives you a million dollars. I pretty much finish projects I've started within two, three, or four years. People are always asking me, "Are you still working on that?" They don't realize how long it takes.

Once you have the money, everything moves quickly, because then you have the resources to hire good people. We've turned films around in six weeks or two months. The Rose Kennedy film was something the Kennedy Family Foundation asked us to do. Because the money was in place, the movie was done in a couple of months. Yet it can take three to five years to complete a really significant feature documentary. Of course, people turn out things for television in a matter of weeks, but it's the difference between a magazine article and a serious book—the storytelling is deeper and more complex.

We bulk up or slim down our creative team depending on the project and deadline. If there's enough money, you pull in a team of three or four, or an additional writer, coproducer, or researcher. I have two or three favorite cinematographers, and I work with the same editors when I can. You share with such people a similar sensibility, similar values, without having to articulate them. The most important thing, besides the work, is to be able to communicate your ideas. Basically you're talking about the project, not each other's egos. I look for enthusiastic people with great sensitivity and intelligence, a sense of humor, and a lot of talent in their particular craft.

STOCK-FOOTAGE LIBRARIES

Being a good documentarian means doing good research. You quickly discover the stock-footage libraries, which exist solely to sell you footage shot by either the networks or independents. In the case of *Return with Honor*, there was amazing 35mm black-and-white footage of American POWs filmed by the North Vietnamese government. It was incredible, like having a second unit shooting 25, 30 years earlier. After the U.S. established diplomatic relations with Vietnam by 1997, we were allowed into their archives. We also found great footage from a pro-Communist news agency in Japan.

A FATAL ATTRACTION FOR YOUR PROJECT

It's great to be able to move people and to have a dialogue with the audience. Not to lecture them, which is probably something I started off doing—as if I had the goods and they didn't. It's a very synergistic relationship.

Still, I have to please myself. Especially in independent films, it's all on your back. I call it having a fatal attraction for your project. It's the only way a project completes itself. You'd better be in love with it, even though afterward you go home and say, "What was that all about?" But during the process of recording and filming, you pretty much have to say it's the greatest. After it's finished, then you can say, "Hmm, let me reevaluate this."

Self-doubt is the enemy. I do trust a kind of gut approach to things. That's either wisdom or foolishness, but it has worked for me so far.

I think the strength is, if you believe then others respond. You have to stay committed to your vision because there are so many distractions along the way.

GET WITH THE DIGITAL REVOLUTION

Start with a great idea and run with it. Go get a couple of books. You don't necessarily have to go to film school, but you can't be totally superficial about things. Making documentaries is quite a demanding process. To do it right takes discipline. A lot of people have been nominated for their first films, but these are often what I call "marinated" films—projects the creators have been working on for a long time.

If you have the resources, hire the best people you can get. If you don't have money, you have to do it all.

Commit yourself. If you really believe in your project, it will happen. But you have to hustle. The money doesn't fall from trees. It's really about doing your due diligence and finding those foundations that are interested. The cable-television world has opened up opportunities, too. There's a lot of need for programming, although it is somewhat formulaic. But it can be a source of income.

The good news is you don't have to wait for a grant. The digital revolution is here. But when you pick up that digital camera, make sure you have a solid story in hand, and have ideas about what the scenes are and who you want in them. I always ask myself how I want to begin a film and how I want to end it. If you just go out and shoot, you're going to have hours and hours of footage to look at in your Final Cut Pro or Avid. I don't like to look at footage that much—it's better to be disciplined in the beginning.

Sing! (2001) Bird by Bird with Annie (1999) Return with Honor (1998) Never Give Up: The 20th Century Odyssey of Herbert Zipper (1996) **AAN, Best Short Documentary Maya Lin: A Strong Clear Vision (1994) *AA, Best Feature Documentary Rose Kennedy: A Life to Remember (1990) **AAN, Best Short Documentary Screenwriters: Word into Image (1984) The Kennedy Center Honors: Biographies (1983) To Live or Let Die (1982) **AAN, Best Short Documentary *AA = Academy Award **AAN = Academy Award Nomination

AVY KAUFMAN
CASTING DIRECTOR

Casting is brilliant when every role works. When you watch a movie and you believe every role, and they are all great, then your casting director has done a superb job.

I STUDIED DANCING IN COLLEGE and took some acting lessons. When I worked with actors, I realized how much they had to offer in telling a story. I started to do casting for an advertising agency. I realized very soon I wanted to work on films because I would bring in actors who were great, but the advertisers only cared about how they looked.

It took me about seven or eight years to get into film. I guess my first break was when John Sayles and his producers Maggie Renzi and Peggy Rajski asked me to work on *Matewan*. John gave me not only the extras to cast, but people who had lines. I would go to West Virginia and find coal miners who could tell a story. I ended up doing three movies with John Sayles.

I don't think casting is anything that can be taught. It's intuition, part of who you are. People ask me, how do you know you've chosen the right actor? I really rely on my intuition. It's almost as simple as whether you believe the actor when he or she reads the part.

I read a script to get the feel of the story and to hear the dialogue. When I read it, I might already be thinking about a certain actor, who could be different from the one the director had in mind. Sometimes I have to show more tapes to the director or producer to try to convince them that the actor I suggested can really do the part.

Sometimes, like with John Travolta in *A Civil Action,* a star is already attached to the movie, so my job is to find the supporting actors. Generally, I cast everybody who has a speaking part. The production company hires another person to cast the nonspeaking parts.

Every film has its own challenges. For *Searching for Bobby Fischer,* the kid had to be a chess player. I went to chess clubs and chess matches and transported myself into that world. For *Save the Last Dance,* the lead had to dance, so I ended up going to dance schools and doing a search. I put an ad in *Backstage*. I had a huge open call—it was on

radio stations—for this one character. We ended up using an actor. I think there is typecasting to a certain extent. A producer might tell me that the actor I suggested doesn't look like a villain. People are surprised to see that a nice person can have a dark streak or a mean way, or that somebody is doing a great job completely out of their "type." It's part of my job to see which actor has that range. On *The Sixth Sense,* the one thing the director didn't want me to find was a blond "actory" kid. When I was doing my auditions, Haley Joel Osment was clearly the best. I called up director M. Night Shyamalan and said, "I know you don't want a blond-haired kid who's acted before, but he is amazing. And he understands the material."

I've been fortunate to work with directors who have great stories to tell. It's really rewarding to help find those people who create the words and the characters that become that message.

FINDING NEW STARS

I'm constantly searching for new faces. Sometimes they go on to become big stars, like Julia Stiles, who went from having one line in a movie that I did to having the supporting role to having the lead.

With little kids it's typecasting, because you cannot change who the kid is—no matter how ambitious the parents are. Like the kid from *Little Man Tate,* I saw him at a school. He came in and had these qualities that could be taken as a renaissance child, and he was very shy. When I like a kid, I always go and meet the parents and talk to them to see how the family will get on with the director and the producer.

What I look for in both actors and the people I hire to work in casting is their openness. The openness brings out a lot of qualities in a person. A lot of the interns I bring on have been actors from NYU or Columbia, wanting to get a feel for the other side. I also have a lot of actors who are readers—they learn a lot by seeing people come in and read for roles.

Divine Secrets of the Ya-Ya Sisterhood (2002)   Don't Say a Word (2001)   A.I. Artificial Intelligence (2001)   Blow (2001)   Save the Last Dance (2001)
State and Main (2000)   Dancer in the Dark (2000)   Keeping the Faith (2000)   The Hurricane (1999)   Ride with the Devil (1999)   Music of the Heart (1999)
The Sixth Sense (1999)   A Civil Action (1998)   The Ice Storm (1997)   Walking and Talking (1996)   Lone Star (1996)   Home for the Holidays (1995)
The Basketball Diaries (1995)   Searching for Bobby Fischer (1993)   Little Man Tate (1991)

Jodie Foster

JODIE FOSTER

ACTOR/DIRECTOR/PRODUCER

Acting, directing, and producing are very different tasks. Of these three, directing is my favorite. It's not just half of you, it's all of you. It's the music I hear, the colors I see, the experiences I've had, the people I've known, the stories that move me. I think it very much reflects who I am as a person. My acting reflects who I'm not. The characters I play are people I could never be, but wonder, "Gee, what would that be like?" My acting is a reflection of my questions about life.

Jodie Foster started her career at age three in a Coppertone commercial. At 14, she was nominated for an Academy Award for her role in Taxi Driver. *After a decade of disappointing movie roles—and a B.A. in literature at Yale—she considered giving up acting.*

WHEN I FINISHED *THE ACCUSED,* I thought I had done a really bad job. It was so over the top. I thought it was going to be the end of me, so I started getting ready to go back to graduate school. But the success of the movie made me rethink my decision. I threw myself headlong back into acting, thinking that I had not given it everything, and that my commitment hadn't been strong enough. If I had the opportunity to work with good material and could be committed, that would make it more satisfying for me.

I used the Academy Award clout from *The Accused* to get a job directing. I found a piece of material that had been offered to me as an actress. When I read it I said, "Yeah, I'll do this as an actress, but you should really hire me as a director." I bugged them about it for another year, until I finally figured out a way to have them finance the film with me directing. So I directed *Little Man Tate.*

LITTLE MAN TATE

I was interested in this idea of the "whiz kid" whose gift of intelligence and excellence becomes his handicap. What's so extraordinary about Fred Tate is not just that he's amazing at math or science, but that he has an emotional precociousness, an emotional depth, that's not only beyond his years but makes his life phenomenally painful to live.

The original script was much more of a black comedy. It would've been a really cute movie. But it struck me that in some ways Fred Tate is a person who is fighting two sides of his personality: the emotional and intellectual sides. I basically grabbed the idea of sort of polarizing this personality into these two women—his mother and Dr. Jane Grierson, the head of the school for gifted children who takes Fred under her wing.

The part that rang true to me was his relationship with his mother—the fact that, even though she was in some ways the reason for his emotional creativity, she would never understand him. No matter how much he loved her, she was never going to be enough. On the other side there was Dr. Grierson, who was intellectually driven, but emotionally scarred, and didn't know how to love him. Fred Tate is a person who is fighting the two sides of his personality. And if he had to choose between the two, he'd die.

This is very true to me, I think. My whole life has been about trying to heal the rift between the two sides of my personality, the feeling too much and the knowing too much. It's not like *Tate* was the story of my life, because it wasn't. It had nothing to do with it. But there's such truth to it somehow as an analogy of my life.

Jodie Foster received an Academy Award for her role in The Silence of the Lambs *and was nominated for her role in* Nell.

Nell was the most challenging experience I've ever had as an actor, because my own personality is so different. It's definitely the best work I've done, although a lot of people will disagree.

My challenge was to show her intelligence and complexity without having the luxury of language. I had to transform myself into somebody who lives with her emotions on the outside, as opposed to someone who has all the trappings of modern culture. How to do that without being completely foolish and over the top, and without having the seams show?

I killed myself doing research for *Nell.* I went to movement classes and studied with an acting coach, and that didn't really do anything. I put a mirror in my house, and I thought, "Okay, I'm going to work it out." When the mirror came to the house, I thought, "This is ridiculous!" I realized that making this role work demanded the least amount of intellectual energy, because I didn't have any options. I just had to drink coffee and do it.

ON PRODUCING AND DIRECTING

I think producing is the worst job on a movie. It's thankless and has no rewards. The only reward you're allowed to claim as your very own is how much the movie made at the box office. And for me, I don't live for the gross of opening weekends. Even if you are the creative force behind the movie, you're not allowed to take credit. It's always a director's film and vision.

Producing is also a very negative job. It's all about what the director or the crew cannot have, what they should not do, or what they should be scared of. And you have to learn how to mitigate that with your personality—how to say no in a way that doesn't feel like no. To me, producing is something I do as a community service to help protect young filmmakers from the claws of corporate filmmaking, or to try and nurture someone else's vision, with absolutely no reward in the end product.

ON DIRECTING AND ACTING

Directing and acting come from two different sides of the brain. Acting at its best is always emotional. Even though you may have control of that emotion, it's always about the emotion and not about the intellectual side of you, which you have to suppress. Ultimately, it's about execution and about performance in one second. As far as I'm concerned, acting is much more stressful than directing could ever be, because for directing you can do your homework and at least come in with something. But as an actor, you never know when you're going to suck, and you don't know when you'll ever find "it."

I don't particularly like to act and to direct in the same movie. It takes some of the joy away from both acting and directing, and I don't necessarily get the best performance out of myself.

DIRECTOR'S ROLE

I try not to work for directors that I don't respect. And *respect* is an even more important word than *like*. But if I end up in a movie that didn't turn out to be what I expected, I will swallow it until the last day of shooting. That's my Protestant work ethic. I don't have a problem with directors who fail from time to time as they are trying to achieve something different; I have a problem with directors who never try anything.

FINDING MATERIAL TO DIRECT

The material that I choose to direct has to be true for me. I need to feel that somewhere it's true in a very essential way, either to who I am or what I've known.

I know directors who work every ten months, and they go, "I don't know anything about scuba diving, so I'd like to make a movie about that." But for me, the film has to be something that I already have a huge emotional commitment to in my life, that reflects something in my life that's really important to me. And if it isn't there initially, I turn it into that.

MOVIES THAT ARE TRUE AND RAW

Having had a company has soured me slightly on films. It's really too bad, because when I didn't read *Variety* and when I didn't know who the head of the studio was, I think I loved movies in a more genuine way. The business of making movies can make you very cynical. I think that's why audiences now have become so cynical. They've been let in on the process of making movies, and they don't have an objective experience in the movie theaters anymore. You can go into a gas station and someone will say, "So, I heard you're opening on 800 screens and moving up to 1,200."

My eternal optimism is that all the bad signs we've experienced in the film business—the quality of movies going down, the global economy affecting the film business, and all that stuff—will eventually lead to some kind of backlash. We'll go back to the seventies, when movies that were true and raw with antiheroes were the top-grossing movies in the country. There'll be more room for high-quality films. But that's just my wish.

FINDING YOUR VOICE THROUGH PERSONAL MOVIES

One of the traps young filmmakers get into is, they are so hungry to direct anything that they direct whatever is handed to them. And they get caught in this cycle where it becomes difficult to search for their own voice. Once you've established yourself as a

director of B-grade genre movies with no substance, you are going to be stuck making those movies for a long time. I am a great fan—and I know this is not particularly popular these days—of the personal movie: things you care about, and what you are about. I feel like those were the films that changed my life. And by making those movies, you figure out what your voice is. You figure out why you like 25mm lenses—what is it about the quality of them that tells your story in a way that other lenses don't? Why do you like ensemble movies as opposed to portraits? What is it about them that reflects your life? And I think that if you don't have the opportunity to ask yourself these questions, you never figure out who you are as a director.

STORIES THAT ARE YOU

There are some stories that are in your blood. When I talk about the movies I directed ten years ago, it still brings tears to my eyes. They are still as provocative a part of my life emotionally as they ever were, because they are true to who I am. Before I directed *Little Man Tate,* I thought I was too young to direct, too young to commit to something for two years. But when you love something, and when you know that it's you, you commit to it for the rest of your life.

Actor: The Dangerous Lives of Altar Boys (2002) The Panic Room (2002) Anna and the King (1999) Contact (1997) Nell (1994) **AAN Sommersby (1993) Little Man Tate (1991) The Silence of the Lambs (1991) *AA The Accused (1988) *AA Stealing Home (1988) Five Corners (1987) The Hotel New Hampshire (1984) Foxes (1980) Freaky Friday (1977) The Little Girl Who Lives Down the Lane (1976) Bugsy Malone (1976) Taxi Driver (1976) **AAN Alice Doesn't Live Here Anymore (1974) Director: Flora Plum (2002, not yet produced) Home for the Holidays (1995) Little Man Tate (1991) Producer: Flora Plum (2002, not yet produced) The Dangerous Lives of Altar Boys (2001) Waking the Dead (1999, executive producer) The Baby Dance (TV, 1998, executive producer) Home for the Holidays (1995) Nell (1994) . Mesmerized (1986, coproducer) *AA = Academy Award **AAN = Academy Award Nomination

JOAN ALLEN
ACTOR

I like my career and the way it has happened, little by little. I look at some of these young actresses, and so much has happened to them at such a young age. I wouldn't have been prepared for that: it would have unnerved me.

I GREW UP IN ROCHELLE, a small town surrounded by cornfields in the northern part of Illinois. My father owned a gas station. From when I was pretty young, I wanted to perform or to be noticed somehow. I took ballet classes and piano lessons, and I even led the hula dance in the spring show for the parents. I was a cheerleader for a couple of years because that was one way of doing some kind of performing. When I didn't make the cheerleading squad in high school, I auditioned for a play and loved it.

Joan Allen studied theater at Eastern Illinois University and Northern Illinois University. She is a founding member of the Steppenwolf Theatre Company.

One great thing about Eastern was that students had the opportunity to start acting on the main stage immediately. Many schools with well-known theater departments make you wait until you're a junior or senior before you can work on the main stage. I wanted to be on stage right away.

I met John Malkovich at Eastern. He transferred to another college, where he and several others began formulating the Steppenwolf Theatre Company. When they moved to Chicago and launched the company, John called and asked me to do a play with them during the summer. I knew I wanted to act, but I didn't have that thing, that "Oh, I've got to get out of this town" or "I'm dying to get to New York!" So it was perfect for me because I went from one family into another.

Steppenwolf was *our* theater, and we knew at the beginning of the season how many plays we were going to be in. We didn't have to audition because plays were selected on the basis of giving good parts to everyone throughout the year. I worked as a secretary during the day to support myself. I completely credit John and Steppenwolf as the rock-solid foundation of my career.

Joan Allen won a Tony Award in 1989 for her Broadway debut in Burn This.

One of Steppenwolf's productions, called . . . *and a Nightingale Sang,* was brought to New York in 1983. It was a dream time for me, and I well up with tears whenever I think back on it. I never imagined that I'd make it to New York, much less that I'd be acting in a play that was so well received. I got an agent because of that play. Also, I met my husband in the play, and we married in 1990. I hadn't done any film work before that, but then I gradually started to get involved with TV and film as well as theater.

LITTLE BY LITTLE

It wasn't until my mid-thirties that I decided I wanted to have a child. I'm always the eternally late bloomer—I'm like the last person to get a fax machine and computer. The name of my company is Little By Little. It used to be a silly little song we sang to our daughter, Sadie, when she was a baby. But when I look back, that's sort of the way my career has been—growing on kind of an even incline. Not radical. Not shooting up or diving down.

Allen was nominated for Academy Awards for Best Supporting Actress for Nixon *and* The Crucible. *Her success in* Nixon *helped her reach a new level of recognition and brought her greater personal satisfaction for film work.*

I think my daughter made me a better actor. She was 16 months old when I did *Nixon,* and I really credit my performance a lot to her. She was very emotional, not an easy baby, and our intense relationship changed me in many positive ways.

It took me years to get used to the technical requirements of film after doing so much stage work. There's no school for acting for a camera; you just pick up information as you go along. I was just trying to hit my mark, stay in focus, and not cause the producers any worry about slowing down the process. It was pretty nerve-racking, but when I finally got it, I started to prefer film to stage. I haven't done a play in over ten years—I will wait for the stage bug to bite me before I commit to one.

INSPIRATION AND RESEARCH

I draw inspiration from the people I work with—writers, directors, other actors, and crew members. I tend to get really inspired from the other performers and their performances—Daniel Day-Lewis is one of my acting idols. I also find inspiration from my friends and family, from the stories I read, or from just observing people walking down the street.

I've played a few real-life people, like Sarah Brady, First Lady Pat Nixon, and journalist Veronica Guerin. I did a lot of research for Pat Nixon, but it was difficult to find material on her because she preferred not to be interviewed. She was more of a mystery to the American public, and that's why I had more license with her than Anthony Hopkins had with Nixon. Fortunately, Barbara Walters had done an eight-minute interview with her, which I watched over and over again to get her physical and vocal patterns correct.

When playing real-life people, I try to find out about the childhood of that person because it informs so much of the type of an adult that person turns into. Pat Nixon was a caregiver from a very young age. She had to nurse her parents through lengthy illnesses, and take care of their home and her brothers. That was a heavy load for someone in her teens. She did have some carefree times in her early twenties, but then, as I saw it, she returned to the caregiver role again after marrying Nixon.

Joan Allen was nominated for an Academy Award for her role in The Contender.

I didn't do a lot of research for the character of Laine Hanson in *The Contender* because we were trying to create a female politician unlike anyone that we had seen before. I met with Senator Blanche Lincoln of Arkansas to learn about the general work and demands of a politician. I watched C-Span and Gerald Ford hearings and did some reading about what goes on behind the scenes in Washington. It was very important for me to make Laine Hanson three-dimensional and not too saintly so that the audience could relate to her predicament and strong stance.

When the Sky Falls, about the Irish crime journalist Veronica Guerin, was a challenging experience. She was a reporter who turned journalism on its ear in Dublin and ended up being brutally murdered by drug lords. Amid the massive amounts of research material that I had on her, the most helpful was an article where people who knew her

from her childhood shared their memories of her. They described her as a charismatic, enthusiastic, dynamic, and fun-loving young girl. That article helped me build a foundation for her character, and I could see that she carried these attributes along with her in her adult life and work.

NO CARDBOARD WIVES/MOTHERS

The Ice Storm, with Ang Lee, was a great experience. When I first saw the movie, I knew within the first 30 seconds that I was going to love it: just the way the film looked with the train coming in, with Tobey Maguire sitting on the platform reading his comic book, the sound, and the music. I think it's an amazing piece of work, and I wish it had gotten more attention.

The older I get, the harder it is to be good. When I was 25, I thought I could play anything. Now I can read a screenplay and know I'm not the best person for this part; someone else should be doing it.

At this point I look for parts that are somewhat different from the ones I've played in the past. If my agent tells me there's a script with a fairly generic mother-wife role in it, chances are I will not read it. I feel that for all the wife-mother roles out there over the past years, I've done the phenomenal ones. I mean, *The Ice Storm, Nixon, The Crucible,* and *Pleasantville*—all those roles were extremely well written and complex.

COLLABORATION

The director-actor relationship is a vital collaboration for me. **I'd be the first to admit that I wouldn't work with a director who made me feel insecure for whatever reasons, intentional or not.** I need to get along and feel a sense of comfort and safety to experiment with the director, in order to successfully do what I do. It's not like he has to be my best friend, but there has to be a sense of mutual respect and trust.

I love the crew, and admire how hard they work. It's so hard to make a movie, much less a good one. You spend so much time with your hair and makeup people. They are the first people you see in the morning, and often the last ones you see at night. They tend to be very sensitive, caring people, who are there when you need them. They know when to sink into the background. In *The Ice Storm,* I had a wonderful hair woman, Aaron Quarries, who would say, "I just see you go away thinking about what you're going to do, and I know I cannot talk to you for awhile." I love that relationship on the set.

Costumes make a tremendous difference in the life of a character. I'll never forget being on the set

of *Nixon,* when Oliver Stone was shooting a scene where hippies were camping out at the Lincoln Memorial. I was there for my still-photo shoot, all done up with my tight little collars. I felt like such an alien walking around in my little outfit, and it made me wonder how these people could possibly relate to each other. The tightness of the dress juxtaposed with the fringe and love beads and long hair of the extras made me comprehend the state of confusion and angst that the country was in at that time. That moment taught me a great deal about the power and meaning of costumes.

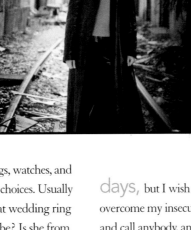

I've worked with wonderful production designers and felt very inspired by the environments they've created. Prop people are incredible. They get very specific about rings, watches, and sunglasses, and present you with an amazing array of choices. Usually the director will come over and we'll contemplate what wedding ring so-and-so would wear. How big should the diamond be? Is she from a poor family? That minutiae is fun to figure out, and really important in fleshing out the character.

Maybe because of all my years in theater, for a long time I didn't really know what to make of the producers of film. I guess I always felt intimidated by them because I thought they were going to fire me or something. Perhaps I saw them as "enemies of the art" for some reason. As I've matured, I've recognized the passion that most of them feel for film, and I've gotten over my silly stigma. Right now I'm coproducing a movie myself, and loving it.

BEING IN PLAY AFTER PLAY

I think that the ingredient that has helped my career the most is experience—being in play after play, whenever I could. I believe you become better at what you do through trial and error. There are great teachers out there that can really help you, but "practice makes perfect" is more my motto—working with talented people, succeeding and failing on certain roles in terms of your personal development.

I did a lot of stage work when I was in my twenties. You didn't have an agent back then—you had an Equity hotline, which would list all the plays they were casting, and some of them were nonunion shows. You would call to audition and get to be seen.

Having persistence and courage is really important. I wasn't overloaded with either of them in my early days, but I wish that had been different for me. I've learned to

overcome my insecurities, little by little. To be able to pick up the phone and call anybody, and share your idea—that quality is really important. This is a business of telling stories, and people are always looking for good ones. Who knows? Yours just might be the next one.

The Contender (2000) **AAN   When the Sky Falls (2000)   Pleasantville (1998)   Face/Off (1997)   The Ice Storm (1997)   The Crucible (1996) **AAN   Nixon (1995) **AAN   Mad Love (1995)   Ethan Frome (1993)   Josh and S.A.M. (1993)   Searching for Bobby Fischer (1993)   In Country (1989)   Tucker: The Man and His Dream (1988)   Manhunter (1986)   Peggy Sue Got Married (1986)   Compromising Positions (1985)   **AAN = Academy Award Nomination

SUSAN SARANDON

ACTOR

The great thing about acting is that, through the people you portray, you are reminded of loss and how fragile your existence is. In real life, we're always fighting the routine and the natural coma we lapse into when we get on track with our lives, and we lose our ability to prioritize. I'm fortunate to sometimes do projects that can remind me of my place in the world and the blessings I've been taking for granted.

I DIDN'T WAKE UP AS A TEENAGER and want to be in the movies; my first motivation was to get out of New Jersey. I got married while in college in Washington, D.C., and my husband, Chris Sarandon, was spotted by an agent while working in the Long Wharf Theatre in Connecticut. Chris asked me to read with him for an audition. I had no interest in acting, and I didn't really make a connection between acting and earning a living.

After we auditioned, the agent Jane Oliver asked to represent me. The first movie I did was *Joe*, John Avildsen's debut film, which became a sleeper hit, kind of an *Easy Rider*. My role was described as the generational prototype of that era, and luckily I had the sense not to try to act, so I came off fairly unscathed in the reviews, and that started my career.

After *Joe*—when I was 20—I was thrown into the world of soap operas. In *A World Apart* I was the girl whom everything happened to. They aged me three years in one season just because my crises got bigger and bigger. Soap operas are a good training ground because you're basically doing theater with all the physical demands of film. You are basically live, except you're working with cameras.

NO TRAINING

I didn't have any training in acting. I don't think you need that—you need life training to survive as an actor. Anybody can act. People hate it when I say this at acting schools, but I think oftentimes acting schools can be damaging. To become an artist, you have to find your voice and what makes you unique. Unfortunately, sometimes, when going through these schools, you surrender your individuality, and the process of becoming who you are is thrown off track. I'm not saying all acting schools are damaging, but you need to choose an environment that makes you feel safe and recognizes your individuality.

In film work it's important to learn how to deal with the variables— how to get the maximum out of yourself under conditions that change. I always compare moviemaking to pioneers going to some unchartered land they all agree on, though the exact destination is yet to be figured out. You circle your wagons against all the adversity you find, with a new set of personalities in a new language every time.

MAKE INTERESTING MISTAKES

I always saw myself as a character actor rather than an ingénue, and I think that's why I'm still doing this. I started out with a lot of people who haven't had longevity. When you start out at 20, it's different than when you come in at 26 or 27 as a leading lady. The transition between ingénue and leading lady is not one that people often encourage.

When starting out, you're allowed a number of failures to learn what you're doing. I think you have to keep making really interesting mistakes—they'll get you on solid ground. The actors that look like they are going to make the transition from ingénue and that have some kind of scope are people like Jennifer Jason Leigh—who started out doing character parts, brave things—even Reese Witherspoon and Natalie Portman. Sean Penn was always a character actor, as was Jeff Bridges. Even though they can play leading men, it helps to look for different parts and be brave in the beginning. I don't think people hold those things against you.

One of my talents is being open to things that cross my path. I'm here because none of my plans worked out. For the first ten years I was acting and trying to figure out who I was, and it was a great way to fight the inertia that is part of my personality.

Susan Sarandon received a Best Actress Academy Award for her role as Sister Helen Prejean in Dead Man Walking.

I found the book and brought it to Tim [Robbins, the director]. I always saw the movie as a love story: for me it was the quest for unconditional love set in a political background. Luckily, Tim and I both had the same perspective, which doesn't always happen. It's all about the point of view, what you show, and how you show it. I once asked a director who has made many good films about his one disaster: he said he just filmed all the wrong scenes.

I think movies have been dumbed down. The success of *Dead Man Walking* makes it clear that audiences are capable of enjoying different kinds of films. It was a very difficult film that should not have been a financial success according to Hollywood standards. How do you explain it? I believe people are eager to find films that are unusual. Whether it's *There's Something About Mary* or *Being John Malkovich*, something that's quirky and interesting, people suddenly try to categorize it and make a bunch of other films like it. But really it's just an original film that someone felt strongly about making, and it shows, and people gravitate toward such films.

My wish would be—and I said this when I was getting an award somewhere in Hollywood, in a room filled with people who green-light projects—if everybody out there did just one project a year, a story they absolutely had to tell, instead of trying to figure out, as we do with our politics, what the polls want, I think it would change the face of Hollywood.

THE PARTS I CHOOSE

Something in the story has to move me. The character has to be a personality I haven't done before, who goes through some kind of a change.

It's also important to know who I'm going to work with and who's directing. And since I've had a family, scheduling is important as well. I can't really take off for Malta in the middle of the school year unless something is so compelling, and I've yet to find something so compelling.

I also like going in for a part that takes two weeks, and not being the one who carries the movie. It just has to be juicy and fun, and something I haven't done before.

Fear plays a part in my decision-making. If there's an element in the story that I'm afraid of, for one reason or another, then I know I'm heading in the right direction.

PREPARING FOR A ROLE

I start by figuring out the arc of the character. If I'm playing a real-life person like [Italian countess] Margherita Sarfatti or Sister Helen Prejean, that makes it easier, because my job as an actor is to be as specific as possible, which leads you to the universal. When you have a book you can read or a video to watch, it makes the job easier. The problem of playing someone you love and who is still alive is that the responsibility can be so terrifying that it can cramp your style somewhat.

I prepare by asking questions in almost an open stream of consciousness. I challenge things a lot, even if I think I have the answer, because sometimes the third thing you find with the director is the thing that works. On both *Bull Durham* and *The Front Page*, there was very little rewriting, so finding activities or the right wardrobe became a way to make the character more specific. Sometimes research helps, sometimes it doesn't. In *The Client*, the more research I did, the more I realized it wasn't helping me. So we worked with Tommy Lee Jones on making our confrontations more substantial by interviewing lawyers and restructuring the plot somewhat.

Finally, when the shooting begins, you just want to listen. I find it helpful to be playful. It's important for me to know the crew and to involve them in the process.

If I'm in a very difficult emotional scene, I'll discuss it with the focus-puller—I'll let him know what might happen so he can work with me. I try to tell the prop department the day before if I might need something, so they have time to get it. You need everybody. The more you involve the crew, the more fulfilling the collaboration is.

For me the difference between film and theater is the difference between masturbation and making love. In film you're trying to get this one little moment all by yourself to happen, whereas in theater you have a relationship with the audience. I suppose you attempt to have that relationship while you're making a film: to have some sense of continuity, to have people there who support you, and when you do move them or make them laugh, hopefully you're on the right track.

EVERY MOVIE IS POLITICAL

It makes me laugh when people call some of the films I've made "political," because I believe every film is political. The question is whether the film enforces stereotypes and clichés or challenges them. The only movies you notice and call political are the ones that challenge the status quo. *White Palace* is a political film, and *The Nutty Professor* is a political film. Anything that encourages people to be the protagonist in their own lives, and maybe in some ways affects their perspective even for two hours, is revolutionary, really.

I'm very interested in the courage it takes to be intimate. People reaching out to each other, whether it's a love story between an 11-year-old and a grown woman, or a story of two women—when and how an individual decides to let her guard down to let someone or something in is an incredibly moving and enabling story to tell.

ROLES MAKE FOR PERSONAL GROWTH

What strikes me about my career is that I just seem to have attracted roles into my life that have been necessary for my personal growth at that time, just as you would attract a lover to your life at some point for whatever it is you're trying to figure out.

I definitely was in some kind of exploration of mortality when I was doing *Dead Man Walking*. I was reading *The Tibetan Book of the Dead*, which really triggered something that made me interested in doing *Stepmom*. I just did *Goodbye Hello*, which deals with loss, violence, and grief in another way. I certainly wasn't looking into the different psyches of moms when I was in my twenties.

FIND YOUR STRENGTHS

There's no set way to do this. Start anywhere. Be a personal assistant to someone, or work on a set. You may start out thinking you want to act and then find out your heart is in a different branch of the business.

You may find you have a visual talent or you want to direct. College is a great hothouse for finding out more about yourself, recognizing your voice, discovering areas that interest you, and coming in contact with people with similar passions.

But if you are afire with the desire to work in this business, don't waste your parents' money. People do go into this business at 18. Find someone who makes you feel safe, someone you can learn from, and if you decide to go to an acting school, find a school that recognizes what about you is unique and builds on that strength. Don't date anyone who makes you feel bad about being successful. Once you get past your mid-twenties and you've learned to weed out people who take time and energy away from you being who you are, things go much quicker. You have more strength, time, and energy. The sign of a good relationship is being productive together.

When I would lose parts, I always made it a point to celebrate. That was my little trick. I would take myself out for a nice dinner. I remember auditioning for the same part every single week for about two months because they could not make up their minds. I was furious. You can only be humiliated if you allow yourself to be humiliated, but certainly the capacity to be humiliated exists. Don't think it only happens to people who are not big stars—many tried-and-true stars have been treated dishonestly and with disrespect as well.

If anyone tells you there's a single plan that works, she's not in the business, because there isn't one way to do it. Work from the inside out. Find your strength. Be humble. Have supportive friends. Live large. Have fun. And go for it while you don't have responsibilities that come later.

Actor: Goodbye Hello (2002)   The Banger Sisters (2002)   Igby Goes Down (2001)   Time of Our Lives (2000)   Joe Gould's Secret (2000)   Anywhere but Here (1999)   Cradle Will Rock (1999)   Stepmom (1998)   Illuminata (1998)   Twilight (1998)   Dead Man Walking (1995) *AA   The Client (1994) **AAN   Safe Passage (1994)   Little Women (1994)   Bob Roberts (1992)   Lorenzo's Oil (1992) **AAN   The Player (1992)   Light Sleeper (1991)   Thelma & Louise (1991) **AAN   White Palace (1990)   A Dry White Season (1989)   January Man (1989)   Sweet Hearts Dance (1988)   Bull Durham (1988)   The Witches of Eastwick (1987)   Compromising Positions (1985)   The Buddy System (1984)   The Hunger (1983)   Tempest (1982)   Loving Couples (1980)   Atlantic City (1980) **AAN   Something Short of Paradise (1979)   Pretty Baby (1978)   The Other Side of Midnight (1977)   The Rocky Horror Picture Show (1975)   The Great Waldo Pepper (1975)   The Front Page (1974)   Joe (1970)   Producer: Baby's in Black (2002)   Stepmom (1998)   Dead Man Walking (1995)   *AA = Academy Award   **AAN = Academy Award Nomination

JEANNINE OPPEWALL
PRODUCTION DESIGNER

In design you ask: What color does the wall want to be? Some directors have a hard time understanding that philosophy. The same way the actors have to go into the character, I believe the designers have to work at the character of the inanimate backgrounds.

I NEVER SET OUT TO BE A PRODUCTION DESIGNER. I never even knew that such a career category existed. I just wanted to tell stories. Whether I wrote them or drew them didn't really matter. I was a person who had an addiction to fiction. I believed in the truth of fiction more than the truth of fact.

Fresh from college, Jeannine Oppewall was hired by legendary designer Charles Eames to do research and build exhibitions. "I am the only person I know who graduated with a straight liberal-arts degree and who got up every morning to use it," Oppewall laughs. The years working for one of the most renowned designers in the U.S. shaped her much-admired and award-winning "less-is-more" vision in production design. She refuses to clutter her movies, opting for a subtle, suggestive style.

I believe in things that are understated. I believe people get more engaged in the story the more they have to fill in with their own imaginations.

A good designer is like a mathematician. You are always looking for the simplest and most efficient way of expressing an idea. After all, it's not words, it's an environment . . . Unless you are portraying a character who is a mess, of course. On *Wonder Boys,* I read the script and said to Curtis Hanson, the director, "I have a terrible feeling I used to live with this guy!"

Certainly there are times when the environment has a separate character. But mainly, the designer's job is to design herself into anonymity. The main thing is for the story to move forward and the characters to move forward. I feel that, when watching a movie, if I'm stopped by some blue jacket in the background that takes me away from the characters and their story, then that blue jacket should not have happened.

PLACES OF POETRY

My work starts with the script and the characters. I think of the script as the designer's client. I start by imagining something about the characters and what places they go through.

A location has to speak to me; it has to have some poetry. I have to be engaged emotionally, at least to some extent. It's intuition, based on a lot of education and experience, and you are paid to use it.

For *The Bridges of Madison County,* the Iowa film commissioner had shown the director three farms, and one of them became the director's favorite. So I went there with the location manager, took one look at it, and said, "I want to leave."

"But this was the director's favorite," he said.

"I don't care," I said. "It doesn't work, it's flat and uninteresting, and I have to convince the director to change it."

So we drove all around and didn't find anything. Then we chartered a helicopter and crisscrossed the county. Twenty minutes out of the airport, I saw it. It was like love at first sight, a farm that had been abandoned for 30 years. Cows were in the front yard, the roof was falling down, the chimneys were gone, the porches were in tatters, there was no staircase inside, the raccoons were living in it, the bees had taken up nests in it, the bats had set layers of guano. So we negotiated to use the place, slowly took it apart and put it back together, rented farm equipment, and completely redid the interior. All because the place had "good bones"—real visual poetry.

SENSITIVITY AND AWARENESS OF WHAT SURROUNDS US

When you are working on a film, and driving around, or walking around, your whole life becomes a funnel for your work. And when your antennas are out, they pick up what they need to. It's an unconscious process, something you internalize. It's like working on a three-dimensional painting: You don't work from left to right, you work little by little, all over the painting, so that the whole picture will make sense.

Sometimes my work is plain, boring, factual research. What does a fishing rod from the 1920s really look like? Sometimes it's looking at images—books, magazines, albums, documentaries—something to feed or inspire you.

Oppewall was nominated for Academy Awards for her work on L.A. Confidential *and* Pleasantville.

When working on *L.A. Confidential,* which had about 95 different sets all over the city, I was driving around Los Angeles with my dashboard

Studying the life of butterflies teaches you how to really look.

You are always scanning the horizon and taking in informa-

tion about what moves around there, or what doesn't belong.

When you become good at it, you can tell from a distance by

the flight pattern what family a butterfly belongs to. It teaches

you sensitivity and awareness of what surrounds us.

filled with Post-it notes about each scene, about the essential ingredients I needed to find for that scene.

THE SKILLS

A production designer has to have a knowledge of art history, architecture, culture, and the basic technical requirements for drafting, sketching, and making models. It's good if you have a background that involves some literature, storytelling, or theater. You need a broad knowledge about a lot, and deep knowledge of some things. I look for people that bring something more to the party, and who get inspired themselves. I don't want to hire sheep. I want to hire people who play well in a sandbox with other people, and have the kind of flexibility to deal relatively easily and cheerfully when things change—because they always do.

I have found that the broader a person's experiences are, the happier I will probably be working with them. For some people, the San Fernando Valley is all they know, and there's nothing wrong with that. But my frame of reference is different, and I need to be able to refer to an architectural period without seeing their eyes glaze over. I found that the most interesting people are the ones who tacked right and left, and for one reason or another just happened to end up in this harbor.

For set decorators, I look for someone whose sensibility is similar enough to my own, someone I am compatible with. Some people are very good at being chameleons; they can get what we need without becoming personally attached to their own choices.

When schedules are tight, and everything constantly keeps changing, the dynamics of the group become very important. That's why it's essential to have a personality that suits the business—to be upbeat and flexible, have reasonably good people skills and a sense of humor that travels.

ABOUT WOMEN AND MEN

A woman as a production designer used to be very rare. It used to be an educated-gentlemen's club. They went to work every day and met their friends.

I like to have an equal balance of men and women in my crew, although I tend to hire younger men rather than older, because of the generation break—older men are not accustomed to answering to a woman. Younger men are more flexible.

Even though I believe that differences from person to person are larger than differences between men and women, I guess there are differences in how we work. Women's working environments tend to be low-key and less political. They tend to want to reach a consensus of opinion somehow. Men are much more respectful of hierarchy. They need to seek their place in a hierarchy, or a pecking order, which doesn't come naturally to me. I'd rather move around and try to achieve an understanding working side by side.

Wonder Boys (2000)   Snow Falling on Cedars (1999)   Pleasantville (1998) **AAN (shared with set decorator Jay Hart; *Pleasantville* was named the Best Designed Picture of the Year by the L.A. Film Critics Association)   L.A. Confidential (1997) **AAN (shared with set decorator Jay Hart)   Primal Fear (1996)   The Bridges of Madison County (1995)   Losing Isaiah (1995)   Corrina, Corrina (1994)   School Ties (1992)   Music Box (1990)   White Palace (1990)   Ironweed (1987)   Light of Day (1987)   The Big Easy (1987)   Desert Hearts (1985)   Maria's Lovers (1984)   Love Letters (1983)   Tender Mercies (1983)   **AAN = Academy Award Nomination

Creating environments is like working on a three-dimensional painting. You don't work from left to right, you work little by little, so that the whole picture will make sense as you try to create a visually and emotionally coherent portrait.

THE ART DEPARTMENT
THE PRODUCTION DESIGNER AND HER TEAM

*The production designer hires and supervises a crew of 15 to 50 people, depending on the movie.
She supervises carpenters, builders, and painters, as well as the set decorator.*

MAKING US BELIEVE that the world on the screen really exists requires the talents and skills of a production designer, who supervises the entire art department. Every building, street, room, and panoramic view, whether existing in the real world or built inside a studio, is the creative responsibility of the production designer and her team.

The production designer starts her work by reading the script and discussing the movie in detail with the director. Then she begins her research, collecting anything and everything that helps her build a coherent portrait, true to the period and characters.

She teams up with the location manager to find locations. "I spend hours in a car with them, just looking, looking, and looking," says Jeannine Oppewall. She imagines where the characters could have lived, where they worked, where they had fun. "The place has to speak to me on some level," says Oppewall. "If not, I will try to convince the director to change the location."

Next she starts building sets and remodeling existing buildings. She supervises carpenters, builders, and painters, as well as the set decorator, who brings in the furniture, drapes, photos on the tables, and pictures on the walls—everything smaller than the building itself. Things have to move rapidly for the film to stay on time and on budget.

She also works closely with the property master discussing the objects—typewriters, surfboards, teacups—that the actors touch in the scene. They all have to fit with the overall art direction and period continuity.

The production designer also collaborates with the costume designer to ensure that background colors and the overall tone of the film are consistent. Do the actors in their costumes fit in, or fight against, the backgrounds being created?

She consults with the camera department about lighting. Should the light be strong or soft? For color, do they want the gold hues of candle-light, the harsh white of a bare bulb, the industrial green tones of fluorescent lighting? If they plan to let a street lamp illuminate a night scene, is the lamp from the correct era?

The art department works months ahead of the actual shoot so that everything is ready when the actors arrive and the cameras start to roll.

"I try to make the environment conducive for the actors to do as good a job as possible," Oppewall says. "Sometimes I send them notes and pictures and invite them for a tour ahead of time. If they do a good job, it reflects well on the rest of us."

She also makes notes with the postproduction department: for example, when to apply "the digital eraser" if her department was unable to physically disguise a period anachronism, or how the places created completely by computers should look.

The key roles in the art department include:

Set decorator—Acquires the furnishings for the environment.

Construction coordinator—Builds the sets ◆ Manages the budget.

Paint supervisor or scenic artist—Creates backdrops ◆ Applies colors ◆ Makes signage ◆ "I tend to like to torture my painters," says Oppewall.

Art director—Works with the production designer side by side ◆ Manages budgets, schedules, and personnel ◆ Supervises those who draw sets, design graphic elements, and do general research.

Location manager—Hired by either the production designer or the producers ◆ "They have one foot heavily in the production camp and one foot heavily in the art camp," comments Oppewall.

Costume designers and property masters are often considered part of the art department, although they are not necessarily directly supervised by the production designer. However, they collaborate closely with the production designer to create a consistent look.

ROSEMARY BRANDENBURG

SET DECORATOR

I provide the surroundings that turn a bare movie set into a seemingly real environment in which actors
do their work: tables and chairs, throw rugs, chandeliers, potted palms, clutter on the floor, family pictures,
unopened bills on the table, a torn window shade—items that support the story and characters.

I STARTED WORKING IN THE THEATER during high school and college, taking stagecraft classes and working in summer stock. After college I worked as a stage manager and prop master at various theaters, supplemented by day jobs. I moved to L.A. in the early eighties and started building a reputation and experience in commercials and feature films.

EVERY BREAK IS A BIG BREAK

If I hadn't met my high school drama teacher, Ted Walch, I never would have found what I love to do. Getting to stage-manage for Paul Newman was incredible. He came to direct a play during my senior year at Kenyon College. I almost fainted when I first met him: growing up, we had posters of him on our walls, for goodness sake!

I got another break when production designer Bill Sandell took a chance and brought me with him from a relatively small but cool film, *Hocus Pocus,* to the much more ambitious *The Flintstones* (the first one). That was my first fully designed project, and it was a real opportunity to shine. I'd say it put me into consideration for bigger-budget films.

The next step was to do something slick, and I got that break working on *The Rock.* I learned a lot on that film about getting beyond the narrative and into pure visual design. Getting the chance to work on *Amistad,* a wonderful period piece, was another huge leap. The most recent break was *Planet of the Apes,* which was about the greatest fun you can have and still get a paycheck. Making up new worlds is always a wonderful challenge.

THE PROCESS

I break down the script, analyze characters, research the period, industry, and style, make ground plans, negotiate for an adequate budget, track the money as it is spent, and hire and supervise set-dressing crews. My job is an exhilarating juggling act, and I love it.

I am hired by the producer, with the blessing of the production designer, who is the head of the design team and my closest colleague. I also cultivate a rapport with the director, whose creative direction we all follow. Financially, I am beholden to the producer—I must spend within limits set by him or her and the studio.

Researching the period and style is probably my favorite part of preparing for a film. Then I move on to furniture layout, color and materials choices, design and ordering of original furniture and decorative objects, drapery design, and selection of rented or purchased set-dressing items.

Timing is an important element. Schedules vary greatly, but on the average feature I usually prepare for two to four months before filming begins, and the shooting period can last another two to four months. We are in different planning and preparation phases at all times. Budgeting is an educated guess, and it can change radically. I keep the producers informed every step of the way.

To find what we need, I shop for fabrics and individual set-dressing items from around the world. Familiarity with prop-house stocks is indispensable, and these vital businesses bend over backwards to help me get the job done. But projects often require arcane specialty items that can't be found in the usual places. I travel a great deal, and surf the Internet as well, in search of odd workshops and unique associations of collectors and dealers. I must be able to produce any object, whether at home, at a studio, or away at some distant isolated location, and often very quickly.

Set decorators are filmmakers first, decorators second. I discuss lighting fixtures with the director of photography, review colors and textures with the costume designer, and discuss each scene with the prop master. I present the director with ideas for conveying character and telling the story through the choices we make. And I always work closely with the production designer and construction departments, because our combined efforts complement the finished product.

Planet of the Apes (2001)   What Women Want (2000)   Coyote Ugly (2000)   Cast Away (2000)   The Thin Red Line (1998)   Psycho (1998)   Small Soldiers (1998)   Amistad (1997)
The Peacemaker (1997)   The Rock (1996)   Outbreak (1995)   Casper (1995)   The Flintstones (1994)   Hocus Pocus (1993)   School Ties (1992)   Everybody's All-American (1988)
The Serpent and the Rainbow (1988)   La Bamba (1987)

Consensus-building is very much a part of the game. We hear a lot about collaboration, and this is very much my stock-in-trade. When the director and production designer aren't seeing eye to eye, sometimes I feel like the monkey in the middle, but it always works out in the end. Creative tension can be used as inspiration.

THE SET DECORATOR

AND HER TEAM

Anyone who wants to be a set decorator needs to be organized, good at management, good with money and budgeting, skilled at design, and interested in sociology, research, and the stuff of life. A successful set decorator has to be resourceful, have excellent communication skills, and be a leader and a collaborator at the same time. It also helps to be fearless, be energetic, and have stamina.

AS FOR CAREER ADVICE, get the best education you can. Sometimes set decoration is taught as a component of production design, but it's better to try to learn about every aspect of filmmaking, as well as to get a broad exposure to design. The following subjects may be particularly useful: drafting; space planning; color theory; photography; history of furniture; decorative arts; art and architecture; film and theater studies. Acting experience will help you when you are inventing character detail. Any computer skills—word processing, spreadsheets, databases, graphics, the Internet—will come in handy.

Work within the theater department wherever you are, and learn everything you can about stage management, script breakdowns, character development, sets, props, and costumes. Work on a student film. You don't have to be enrolled in a film class to help out, and it's a great way to build experience. Check the bulletin boards in film, theater, and communications departments at local colleges and universities.

Volunteer as a P.A. (production assistant) in an art or production department. Get paid if you can, of course. Or work at a prop house to learn styles, periods, scheduling, and budgeting. It's also a terrific way to meet set decorators and crew people.

Become a keen observer of how people live and work within their environments. Take notes and photos to create your personal research files. Spend time at flea markets and swap meets. Get to know antique dealers, visit design showrooms, fabric stores, and specialty shops, and begin compiling a personal "sourcebook."

The set decorator makes it happen by using the following skilled crew members:

Lead person—Leads the set-dressing crew day-to-day • Organizes prop pickups and returns • Helps coordinate fabrication projects • Coordinates loading and off-loading of delivery trucks • Places set

dressing according to the set decorator's specifications • Tracks paperwork • Manages crew timesheets.

Set dressers (a.k.a. "Swing Gang")—Load and off-load trucks • Dress and strike sets • Clean set props and furniture • Repair and hang fixtures and switch plates • Attach wires and pipes to set walls • Assist with minor modifications to set-dressing items • Set interior greens if no greensman present • Organize set-decorating storage warehouse.

Buyer/shopper—Shops for individual items as directed • Assists with research and presentations • Assists with dressing and striking sets.

On-set dresser—Works with the prop master on the shooting set to manage the set dressing • Represents the set decorator on the set • Relays changes made after the set decorator has opened the set • Supervises set-dressing materials, keeping props safeguarded and clean • Sets dressing back to original position for camera resets • Adjusts set pieces to camera • Helps maintain continuity.

Drapery person—Helps find appropriate drapery fabrics as directed • Measures windows and areas for linens and area rugs • Supervises any additional drapery personnel • Supervises fabrication and installation of draperies, including awnings and door coverings • Organizes cleaning, pressing, and installation of table and bed linens • Strikes and returns purchases to warehouse and rentals to studios.

Floorcovering person—Assists the drapery person • Picks up and installs flooring and carpeting, baseboards, and area rugs • Supervises repairs and cleaning • Strikes and returns purchases.

Upholsterer—Assists the drapery person • Upholsters new or used set pieces and furniture in fabrics supplied by the set decorator.

When needed, the set decorator's team may also include additional craftsmen, such as carpenters, prop-shop personnel, painters, sculptors, mold makers, metal workers, plumbers, sign, flag, and banner makers, and fixture electricians.

Ruth Carter

RUTH CARTER

COSTUME DESIGNER

Big egos are the hardest part for me to accept in this business. I feel like I am an idealist, and I want people to want what's best for the movie. When egos get involved, it's not about content anymore, it's about business.

I ATTENDED THE HAMPTON INSTITUTE (now Hampton University) in Virginia. After I graduated, I packed my stuff in the back of my Volkswagen and drove across the country for an internship at the Santa Fe Opera. I worked 17-hour days for $50 a week, and lived with five roommates. But it didn't matter then—I loved what I did, and I wasn't afraid. When you are young, be bold, and don't be afraid. You have to have self-motivation and drive, and you have to be willing to take the chance.

I got a job at LATC [Los Angeles Theatre Center] as a dresser, sitting backstage in the dark, doing fast changes. I'd team up with the designers who came through, and I'd do all their dyeing or aging. They started requesting me, and I started asking them questions about film.

"THIS IS THE MAN OF YOUR DREAMS"

I was hired to do costumes for this little dance studio in South Central. Spike Lee was among the first ones to come and see their performance. I didn't know him—he had just finished *She's Gotta Have It*. We hung out after the performance, and Spike suggested that I sign up for one of the senior thesis projects at USC or UCLA to get some experience on how to work on a set.

His film went to Cannes and was a huge hit. He called me up and said, "This is the man of your dreams." And I said, "Who's this? Billy Dee Williams?" "No," he said. "It's me, Spike, and I want you to design my next movie."

Ruth Carter's career in motion pictures began in 1988 on Spike Lee's School Daze. *She went on to design the costumes for all of the Spike Lee movies*

thereafter, including Do the Right Thing, Jungle Fever, Malcolm X, *and* Summer of Sam.

You should have formal training because costume designing is not only about fashion, nor is it only about shopping for clothes. You need to know costume history and how garments are made.

WARDROBE IS PART OF THE STORY

People skills are important as well because the costume designer has to be very intimate with the actors. Actors need to feel comfortable in what they're wearing and look great. At the same time, the wardrobe is part of the story, part of the personal transformation of the character, and the clothes have to help the actors become the character they are playing.

Also, clothes have to be in sync with the general color palette laid out by the production designer, which is all part of the director's vision.

The costume department is looked on as the lowest on the totem pole. It's not as glamorous as being a production designer who builds sets, or a D.P. with his cameras, but it's equally important. It's still considered below the line, and it shouldn't be.

Ruth Carter is a two-time Academy Award nominee for her work as a costume designer on Malcolm X *and* Amistad.

I have been painted with the Hollywood brush, which makes me golden in color. So I don't go to Europe to do smaller budget movies, although I often entertain the idea of taking off and doing something completely different.

I Spy (2002) Baby Boy (2001) Doctor Dolittle 2 (2001) Bamboozled (2000) Shaft (2000) Love & Basketball (2000) Summer of Sam (1999) Down in the Delta (1998) Amistad (1997) **AAN Rosewood (1997) Crooklyn (1994) Cobb (1994) What's Love Got to Do With It (1993) Malcolm X (1992) **AAN The Five Heartbeats (1991) Jungle Fever (1991) Mo' Better Blues (1990) Do the Right Thing (1989) I'm Gonna Git You Sucka (1988) **AAN = Academy Award Nomination

TRISH GALLAHER GLENN
PROPERTY MASTER

As a child growing up in Texas, seeing To Kill a Mockingbird *was a powerful experience. Shown in the opening shots, Boo Radley's cigar-box treasures—a pocket watch, coins, marbles, and the carved figures—were all so telling. Props are a critical part of the story and help reveal a character to the audience. That's what makes my job so fascinating.*

WHEN I WAS STARTING OUT, I tried to do projects that appealed to me—a filmmaker or script I admired, or a period movie that would broaden my experience. Directors and producers don't necessarily look for people who have worked on blockbuster hits. They look for someone who has worked on interesting projects, hoping that person can bring another point of view to their film.

PROPS AND CONTINUITY

The propmaster is responsible, in a technical sense, for everything the actors pick up and touch in a film—newspapers, pens, cell phones... the minutiae of life. For example, in the state-dinner sequence in *The American President,* my crew and I prepared hundreds of specially designed white chocolate desserts, printed menu cards, manufactured special double-wicked candles, and outfitted Secret Service agents, White House waiters, and the entire press corps. We used photographs of Michael Douglas and Annette Bening dancing to create prop newspapers for later scenes in the film.

Once the shooting has begun, we are responsible for all of the continuity in the art department—the furnishings as well as hand props. Since films are shot out of order, we take Polaroids to make sure that items match from shot to shot. Every detail matters—the angle of the pen on the desk, how many bites of pie the actor has taken, or the order that the clothes get thrown into a suitcase. We also take pictures of how the actors carry their briefcases, tools, weapons, or badges. And if there's a scene with a candle burning, we make sure it continues burning from the same length, even after 30 takes.

REALITY DETECTIVE

My work starts two to three months prior to shooting. After listing every prop in the script scene by scene, I start my detective work. Libraries, art bookstores, and newspaper archives... I research exhaustively the script's subject matter. For period films, I study old props from paintings and old photographs. However, the best information comes from real people—technical advisors. For *Murder By Numbers,* we visited the Hollywood homicide office, looked at photos of real crime scenes, and asked detectives how they do their jobs.

The Internet has really changed my work. What might have taken weeks to source out ten years ago can sometimes be found in a couple of clicks. I also buy props from flea markets and stores, rent props, and have custom props made. We always have at least two of every item, in case one gets broken or lost. Or we may prepare 60 steaks for the one that you see the actor eat.

It's important to know how the props are used and handled, which is not always obvious, especially with period movies. For the blood-transfusion scene in *Bram Stoker's Dracula,* we found an early transfusion setup in England, duplicated it in our special-effects shop, and then taught the actors how to use it on set.

I get into the smallest of details to help the actors become the characters they play. I meet with the actors to select their rings, watches, sunglasses, briefcases, and the things they carry in their pockets, even if they're never going to be seen by the camera. For Jack Lemmon in *Tuesdays with Morrie,* we made lap blankets of the exact fabric that the real Morrie Schwartz had owned.

The prop master was traditionally a man's job in Hollywood. It was one of those crafts that fathers passed on to their sons. Now that women work in every aspect of the industry, those stereotypes have broken down. I've always felt that as a woman, and now as a wife and mother, I bring something extra to every job I do.

While finally working with Gregory Peck on *Other People's Money,* imagine my thrill when he pulled me aside to say, "Happy birthday, Scout!"

 Murder By Numbers (2002) Miss Congeniality (2000) Tuesdays with Morrie (2000, TV) The Out-of-Towners (1999) Paulie (1998) Ghosts of Mississippi (1996) Multiplicity (1996) The American President (1995) Speechless (1994) Speed (1994) Gypsy (1993, TV) Flesh & Bone (1993) The Vanishing (1993) Bram Stoker's Dracula (1992) Other People's Money (1991) The Doors (1991) White Palace (1990) Dad (1989) In Country (1989) Far North (1988) The Milagro Beanfield War (1988) Less Than Zero (1987) Desert Hearts (1986)

LISA RINZLER
CINEMATOGRAPHER

My job is to enhance and embellish the director's vision. Before I come onto the scene, they've already lived with the story they want to tell for months, maybe years. I try to understand their vision, bring my own ideas to the table, and offer, hopefully, what they want—and then some. It's never about recording; it's about collaborating and going to the next level.

I BEGAN AS A PAINTING STUDENT at Pratt Institute in Brooklyn, but I wasn't a very good painter. Painting eventually led me to film—I needed to add motion to the mix of light and color—and I switched from Pratt to NYU. As soon as I got into film, I knew I wanted to shoot, so I shot as many student films as I could. After graduation, I worked briefly as an electrician, then as a second and first camera assistant, and finally moved into shooting.

When I started out, cinematography was predominantly a man's field. I never allowed myself to focus too much on the gender issue. I really wanted to light and shoot, so I focused on that.

The great thing about shooting is that it's a marriage of the technical and the intuitive. It's not a science. There's something far greater involved, and it doesn't have to do with being male or female. It has to do with you, and what you bring to it.

On feature films I worked with Fred Murphy, who became my unofficial mentor. He had me diagram his lighting, which was invaluable to me—not that I light similarly, but observing him was educational. The other thing he taught me was how to exist on the set under pressure, and not to become impatient or ragged. I've learned a lot from people who have strong commitments and are able to balance personal life and career.

PREPARATION IS ESSENTIAL

Research is the foundation of my work. I study photographs, paintings, and other films. I just learned platinum palladium printing, which is a technique from the 1850s. While everybody's moving toward digital, I was moving backward. Research and preparation are essential, even though by the time you get to the set, they're not on your mind any-

more. Once you're on a set, serendipity takes over. Planning in two dimensions gives way to the third dimension of actually being there with all the elements of the moment. I rely on the preparation in order to be able to embrace the serendipity. It's that combination of heading toward a vision with enough openness and fluidity to seize the moment.

I've done many experimental movies. *In the House* was about teenagers in a psychiatric hospital. *World without End* was a lyrical documentary about "end-timers," people who thought the end of the world was coming at the millennium. I love those projects because they're personal, and working within the experimental form provides a freedom to try things.

Dead Presidents was the first time I worked with a bigger budget and saw what that could bring. There wasn't as much teeth-pulling to get the tools we needed, in terms of equipment and production design elements.

TRANSCEND AND TRANSPORT THE VIEWER

But whether big or small movies, the key for me is to be motivated by the subject and the director. It's also important to me not to do the same film over and over. I would be very sorry if every film I shot looked the same.

As for whom I hire, I look for people who are technically excellent at their jobs, and who I'd like to be around 14 hours a day. It's the time-money factor. We're trying to make something that isn't just recorded material, that isn't mundane, that transcends and transports the viewer. That's the goal.

Love, Liza (2001)   Pollock (2000)   Buena Vista Social Club (1999, New York scenes)   World without End (1999)   Three Seasons (1999)   In the House (1997, short)   Black Kites (1996, short)   Trees Lounge (1996)   Dead Presidents (1995)   Lisbon Story (1994)   Menace II Society (1993)   Guncrazy (1993)   Death by Unnatural Causes (1991, short)   True Love (1989)   No Sense of Crime (1987)   Reverse Angle (1982, short)

KERRY LYN McKISSICK

SCRIPT SUPERVISOR

I oversee the continuity, help actors with their dialogue and matching action, and keep a log on everything that has to do with the shooting of a film. My script log, also called "the bible," goes to editors to use as a reference guide through the editing. I'm the overall eyes, and everything coordinates through me, so I truly feel like being in the epicenter of moviemaking.

AFTER I GRADUATED FROM HIGH SCHOOL, I heard about Sherwood Oaks Experimental College, where working professionals in the film industry came to teach. I didn't know anybody in the business, so I thought this school would be a good place to start. I took just about every class they had, among them script supervising.

I had worked as an assistant to a clothing designer who began working on films, and eventually I started to design costumes on my own for small-budget movies. One night, after 22 hours of shooting, I scribbled down some notes for the script supervisor and gave them to her the next day. She said they were pretty good, and asked whether I wanted to learn script supervising. So she trained me on that film. I started to prefer script supervising to costume design because I got to be in the center of the shooting and really learn how a movie is made.

DIRECTOR'S ADDED MEMORY

I'm hired three weeks before the shooting starts. First I do a continuity breakdown—I go through the script, and if scene number 204 says that a character has a cane, I make sure he has that cane in all the scenes leading up to that.

Once we are shooting, I keep a log on every detail of every shot that is made. I time every shot. I name every shot, and give it a letter that goes on a slate. I keep the camera and sound departments in sync on what take we're on, and on what take the director wants printed.

I'm by the director's side all day long because it's important to hear his comments. I work closely with the first assistant director and the cine-matographer to keep track of the intention he wants in a scene. Perhaps the whole take wasn't good, but there was something in particular he liked about the performance or the camera move, or things that went particularly well or poorly with sound, makeup, hair, wardrobe . . . I record the notes made by all departments.

Matching action is about remembering the moves the actors make throughout the scene—when they cross their legs, or toss their hair behind their shoulders. I make sure they repeat that action exactly the same way from take to take; if there are differences, I inform the director of them. Ultimately it's the director's decision whether it has to match or not. But it's my job to keep track, so that in editing they're aware of it when they cut from an actor's close-up to their medium shot to their master shot.

Sometimes the rehearsal has taken place months before, so I share my staging and temperament notes with the actors to help them remember the ideas they began with.

FILM FAUX PAS

Luckily, I still have the ability to go to the movies like a civilian, and not notice the continuity mistakes. On behalf of script supervisors every-where, I will say that some continuity faux pas are our fault, and some aren't. A director may choose to use the take that doesn't match because he loved the performance. And in the end, it's the performance that matters, and that's how it should be.

HOW TO BECOME A SCRIPT SUPERVISOR

You have to love organization because the details and the paperwork are the basics of the job. But once you've mastered those things—and it takes a while before you do—they become second nature. And then you can concentrate on the more challenging parts of the job.

There are classes that teach the fundamentals of script supervising. Try to work on student films, at AFI (American Film Institute), for example. Try to hook up with a script supervisor that you can work with on second unit. Call productions that you know are starting up. Send resumes. Eventually you'll move up to a feature of your own.

Murder By Numbers (2002) Bandits (2001) Galaxy Quest (2000) The Story of Us (1999) True Crime (1999) Beloved (1999) Bulworth (1998) Ghosts of Mississippi (1996)
The Chamber (1996) The American President (1995) Two Bits (1995) In the Line of Fire (1993) A Few Good Men (1992) For the Boys (1991) City Slickers (1991) Misery (1990)
After Dark, My Sweet (1990) When Harry Met Sally (1989) Everybody's All-American (1988) Colors (1988) Who's That Girl? (1988) Hollywood Shuffle (1987) La Bamba (1987)
At Close Range (1986) Purple Rain (1984)

Betsy Magruder

BETSY MAGRUDER

FIRST ASSISTANT DIRECTOR

My job is a combination of organizational skills and people skills. Both abilities are necessary because I work with so many different personalities. You have to have enough of an ego to have a presence on the set, but not so much that you think it's your movie.

I HAVE A B.A. IN FILM AND VIDEO COMMUNICATIONS from Stanford University. After school I started working for free as a production assistant. It was while I was working on a little TV movie that I saw an assistant director for the first time. I remember turning to a friend and saying, "That's what I want to do."

The first assistant director is hired by the director. She usually joins a production 8 to 12 weeks before shooting starts.

Planning is an essential part of my job. I analyze the script, plan and coordinate the shooting schedule, deal with location availability and the actors' schedules, decide what's needed for any given scene, and then make this information available to everybody. I collaborate with the production designer, the costumer, the key grip, the gaffer, the prop master, and all the other department heads to make sure that everything will happen, and happen at the right time.

THE HUB OF THE WHEEL

Once we are shooting, I'm the person who's in physical control of the set. If possible, I prefer to stand right by the camera. I'm actually the person who says, "Hold traffic," or "Here we go," or the one who gets everybody ready and then says, "Roll camera." It truly feels to me like I'm the hub of the wheel. I think that's what attracted me to this job. If somebody needs something, they'll often come to me first. It's a great part of my job because I love being involved in everything.

The person I work most closely with is the director. I'm there to take the pressure off so the director can concentrate on his or her craft. But with creative things, my opinion doesn't count. It's the director's movie, and it's not my place to skulk around and question the director's decision.

THE SET HIERARCHY

In terms of set operations, I'm right below the director and the D.P. (director of photography). I always like to think it's more of a triarchy, as opposed to a hierarchy, but it's definitely a hierarchy.

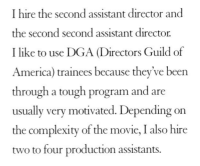

I hire the second assistant director and the second second assistant director. I like to use DGA (Directors Guild of America) trainees because they've been through a tough program and are usually very motivated. Depending on the complexity of the movie, I also hire two to four production assistants.

I look for people with a sense of humor and who are extremely energetic. The second assistant director is a long-suffering job, but a key element. They have to multitask like crazy, be able to do 50 things at once, and politely answer calls at 3 a.m. requesting directions to the set.

My advice would be to be open to starting at the bottom, and be enthusiastic about everything. Show that you love to solve problems and be in the thick of it. Be confident that it will lead you somewhere—but not by tomorrow. There has to be a foundation for the skill and the craft, and you don't build that overnight.

A View from the Top (2002) The Man Who Wasn't There (2001) O Brother, Where Art Thou? (2000) Anywhere but Here (1999) October Sky (1999) A Thousand Acres (1997) If These Walls Could Talk (1996, TV, segments "1952" and "1974") Jumanji (1995) Safe Passage (1994) The Pagemaster (1994) The Rocketeer (1991) Vital Signs (1990) Honey, I Shrunk the Kids (1989) Casual Sex? (1988) Soul Man (1986) Sid and Nancy (1986) Black Moon Rising (1986) Trancers (1985) The Terminator (1984) Repo Man (1984)

CHRISTY SUMNER

SPECIAL-EFFECTS TECHNICIAN

I love my job because every day is different. One day I could be doing nothing more than providing a little bit of wind on a palm tree outside a window on stage, and the next day I'll be 30 feet underwater, hooking up hydraulic hoses on a gimbal.

I CONFESS: I WAS A TOMBOY, and as a little girl I was always getting into trouble playing with fire. Once I persuaded my friend to allow us to put a campfire in her backyard. Her mom wasn't home, but she reluctantly agreed. You can imagine the horror on her mother's face when she came home and saw two seven-year-old girls sitting calmly around a nice, roaring campfire.

Fast-forward 20 years: I get an opportunity to assist in a film production. When I'm on the set, I see the special-effects crew. They are doing the most minuscule effect, flipping a beer-bottle cap in the air for a commercial, but I know right then that that is exactly what I want to be doing.

Christy Sumner didn't know of any other women working in the field, but she kept asking every special-effects person she could find about how to get into the business.

There's no school to learn special effects. It's all on-the-job training. You have to find somebody who's willing to give you a shot. You have to prove to that person that it's the thing you want most in the world, because your energy level, your enthusiasm, and your commitment have to be top-notch. It can't be anything below that—there are so many people who want to do this job.

In the beginning, you're doing all the grunt work—cleaning up after everyone, lifting all the heavy equipment. You're basically looking over everyone's shoulders, learning what they're doing. Then, when you get to go on set and do your first effect in front of the camera, and no one's there to make sure you don't screw up, then you know you've sort of arrived because somebody trusts you enough to perform in front of the camera.

THE JOB

Our job involves any object that wouldn't normally move on its own at any given time. Say a picture frame falling off a wall on cue. Or any type of weather element—wind, rain, or snow. Any kind of pyrotechnic, an explosion of any kind. When you see a fire in a fireplace, a special-effects person is doing that. We also take care of bullet hits, or bullets landing anywhere.

You need to know a little bit of electronics, carpentry, chemistry, physics, and a lot of math. Had I known my ideal job would involve all the fields I despised in school, I would've paid more attention.

Figuring things out mechanically is 90 percent of the job. How can you make a car roll over at this point, or a vase fall over exactly on cue? We do lots of research and experimenting, and test, test, test. We also consult experts, for example, structural engineers who can calculate how much weight you can put on a structure, and how to distribute the weight evenly.

To create the flood for *Dante's Peak,* I worked on the quarter-scale miniature of the river, which was 25 feet across. The top dump tank was on scaffolding 50 feet off the ground, with almost a million gallons of water inside, eight pounds per gallon. We needed to figure out how to let the water come down from the top tank, knock a bridge out, and get back to the top tank again within 20 minutes. Originality is the criterion for brilliant special effects. When someone comes up with an effect in which the danger factor is astronomical, the planning that goes into producing that effect is just mind-boggling.

WHAT YOU NEED TO SUCCEED

What you definitely need is an even temper, a cool, calm head in the face of adversity. The hours are extremely long—I've worked 25-hour shifts; sometimes you do all-night shifts. You have to be able to stay alert under those conditions, especially when you are doing pyrotechnics or something where one little slip-up could mean somebody's life or limb.

You become almost overly conscious of safety. The saying goes, "Ask yourself right before you push the button, 'Okay, what am I gonna tell the judge?'" Sometimes so many things are going on in your mind, and it can be such a mad rush, it's easy to forget something vitally important. You really have to settle yourself and remain calm.

My advice to anyone wanting to work in special effects is to visit film sets, go to music-video houses, and check out commercial houses. Tell them you are willing to work for free as a production assistant. And through that, you should do exactly what I did: talk to as many people as you possibly can. People will sense your enthusiasm. That was one thing I struggled with: I didn't want to nag people; I didn't want to be a pest. But you know what? This is my career—this is my life. What's more important: succeeding in your career or making somebody feel like you're being a little bit of a pest?

Getting a pyrotechnician's license is also part of the job. There are three different levels. A three card can do only fireplaces or small propane fires. A two card can do sparks and other things of that nature, along with other devices. The one card can pretty much do any explosions and the larger effects.

When visual effects came into the picture, everyone in special effects got really scared and started to wonder whether they were going to have jobs in five years. I think it's given us even more work because the audience is now more demanding as a result of the increased sophistication in the effects. They aren't going to settle for just a computer-generated effect. Ninety percent of the time, it's still more cost-effective for a producer to do a physical effect, as opposed to a computer-generated effect. And the movies that have more computer-generated effects also have physical effects tied into them. So the addition of visual effects has definitely helped our field.

 Life As a House (2001)   Joe Dirt (2001)   The Hollywood Sign (2001)   What Lies Beneath (2000)   House on Haunted Hill (1999)   Almost Heroes (1998)   American History X (1998)   No Code of Conduct (1998)   Dante's Peak (1997)   Jackie Brown (1997)   The Winner (1997)   Bulletproof (1996)   Mad Dog Time (1996)   Set It Off (1996)   From Dusk Till Dawn (1996)   Bordello of Blood (1996)   Angus (1995)   Demon Knight (1995)   Four Rooms (1995)   Mortal Kombat (1995)   The Mask (1994)

While trying to get established in this field, be willing to sacrifice your personal life for your career. Just don't let it go on forever, because this industry can suck the life out of you so quickly that if you don't keep the balance, you'll go crazy. Once you're established, be willing to sacrifice your career for your personal life.

Ve Neill

MAKEUP ARTIST

Personality is a big part of being a makeup artist. We are the first people actors see in the morning. We have to be level-headed, good-humored, not hungover, and not in a bad mood, because any negativity will definitely transfer to them. When the actors get to the set, they have to be not only looking great but feeling great.

FROM ABOUT AGE 3 TO 12, I lived next door to a makeup man. Every Halloween, he would make his daughter and me up, and I would say, "Mr. Lotito, I wanna do what you do when I grow up." Back then, women were not makeup artists—they were hairdressers or body-makeup artists.

Flash forward about ten years: I had an antique clothing store that was frequented by rock 'n' roll bands looking for costumes. I started making clothes for this one band, along with dyeing their hair and doing their makeup. One day they told me, "We want to have pointed ears and big heads, you know, sci-fi stuff." I went to this science-fiction convention where all these guys were dressed up like characters from *Planet of the Apes*. I asked them if they could help me. They said, "Sure. If you just buy us the stuff, we'll make it in our garage." It didn't take long for me to realize that I had a knack for prosthetic application. I eventually worked my way into getting jobs in little movies here and there.

Ve Neill met Fred Phillips, who had done makeup on TV's original Star Trek *series. "Freddie called me up, and asked me to do the first* Star Trek *movie with him and his daughter Janna. It was my first big film, and I never stopped working after that," Neill recalls.*

You have to do what the director wants, but you put your expertise into it. Two of the most challenging films I've done were for Steven Spielberg. On *Amistad,* we had to come up with a technique that would create scars and bloodwork, yet would be impervious to cold, water, heat, and rubbing. The actors were in water all the time, and we were shooting in cold, cold weather. Almost all the scar material is a plastic-based product; if it gets cold, it cracks and pops loose. We were testing for about the first four weeks—testing as we were shooting, which is very difficult. We finally did come up with something that stayed on really well and looked really great.

The second big challenge was on *A.I. Artificial Intelligence.* Steven wanted to create a look on a human being that would replicate an artificial being, and the skin had to have a plastic feel with a satin sheen to it. The materials we use to make somebody shiny are either oil-based products—which means nothing's going to stay on with them—or a plastic sort of material, which will crack, wrinkle, peel, and do all of these things when an actor's face starts moving.

We tested for weeks, but none of the products worked properly because as soon as the actors started talking, you could see funny wrinkles in their faces. We tried every type of layering, every type of sealer and product we could find. Finally, I went to a makeup artist named Kenny Myers. He made us a clear gloss-sealer that did not crack and that created this really great sheen. Steven said, "Yeah, that's it. That's what I want."

Ve Neill has been nominated for the Best Makeup Oscar six times, and has won three Academy Awards.

Makeup is brilliant and deserves an Oscar when it accomplishes exactly what it's supposed to do: when it looks right to the eye, when it moves and looks realistic, when it re-creates a mythological character or historical likeness that actually works, or when it accurately captures the effect of an old person without looking like a rubber face or somebody in makeup.

For me it's pretty difficult to watch a film if it's got a bad makeup job because all I can see is the bad makeup, or the bad wig, or whatever it is. It can be very distracting.

NETWORK AND LEARN THE SET ETIQUETTE

First of all, if you want to be a makeup artist it's very important to cultivate an even-keeled temperament. Being funny is always good. I like people who are not too dramatic. Know that there will be difficult times when you need to stay focused and do your job even when other people's tempers flare up.

You can learn to do makeup by going to a specialized school, or you can start out in college or community theater. If you're too young to be enrolled in college, ask if you could work for their productions. You have to have stick-to-itive-ness. If you have to work for free, do it.

Once I worked with an act-ress who kept looking at the mirror between every take. The director just got sick of it and took the mirror from her. He pointed at me and said to her, "You know what? She is your mirror now!" I thought, "What a good way to put it!"

If you have to assist somebody and carry their stuff, do that. And while you're in school, start networking. The important thing is to get out there, get into the swing of it, start meeting people, see what they have to offer. If you meet anybody who knows someone you want to be involved with, call them and say, "Hey, can I just come and watch?" There's a whole set etiquette you need to learn. At first, you never know when to do touch-ups. You're always running in at the wrong time. They're about to roll, and you're in there powdering, or going in and touching up people who are not on camera, or talking when you shouldn't be. You have to learn all that stuff.

The trust between you and the actor comes with time. A lot of actors are not happy unless you're always in there touching them. I feel that my time is in the trailer, and I do not go out and touch actors unless they need to be touched. Acting takes a lot of concentration—once they get on the set, actors have to retain their character, their composure, their hysteria, or whatever. If you're constantly going in there and touching them, it's going to break their concentration, which is not the way to get a good relationship going. Eventually, the actors learn to respect your judgment.

Death to Smoochy (2002)   A.I. Artificial Intelligence (2001)   Blow (2001)   Dr. Seuss' How the Grinch Stole Christmas (2000)   Galaxy Quest (1999)   Man on the Moon (1999)   Stigmata (1999)   Amistad (1997)   Batman & Robin (1997)   Gattaca (1997)   Mars Attacks! (1996)   The Evening Star (1996)   Matilda (1996)   Batman Forever (1995)   Cobb (1994)   Junior (1994)   Ed Wood (1994) *AA, Best Makeup   Mrs. Doubtfire (1993) *AA, Best Makeup   Rising Sun (1993)   Hoffa (1992) **AAN, Best Makeup   Batman Returns (1992) **AAN, Best Makeup   Curly Sue (1991)   Hook (1991)   Edward Scissorhands (1990) **AAN, Best Makeup   Dick Tracy (1990)   Flatliners (1990)   Beetlejuice (1988) *AA, Best Makeup   Big Top Pee-wee (1988)   Cocoon: The Return (1988)   The Lost Boys (1987)   *AA = Academy Award   **AAN = Academy Award Nomination

DEDE ALLEN

EDITOR

I was never afraid of breaking the rules. I knew my craft well, and I knew my tools, and I liked to try a lot of things. I had to keep telling my sound editors, "Don't change that. It's not out of sync. That's the way I want it."

I WAS A REAL MOVIE HOUND AS A KID. I grew up during the Depression, and in those days you could go to two features for ten cents. I never had much homework, so I would go off to the movies every day.

By the time I got to college, the war was on, and I decided I wanted to work in the movies. I came to Hollywood and stayed in one of those little Martha Washington, women-only hotels and started looking for a job as a studio messenger. Of course, there were no women messegers at that time, but because of the war they were beginning to consider taking some on. Faith Hubley and I were the first girl messengers at Columbia Pictures. Just the idea of being where the movies were made was a thrill. I got to know every department and what they did. It took me ten months, but finally I was hired into sound effects because the head of sound said, "I'm hiring you to get rid of you because you are such a pest." I started apprenticing in the library. I got to be an assistant, and then sound-effects editor.

In 1950, Dede Allen moved to New York. She worked for a commercial house, Filmgraphics, and learned everything about opticals.

I was also a script supervisor for a while. Everything you learn helps you. By the time I got my first break, I was totally trained. Director Robert Wise took a chance on me; I was the first woman editor he ever worked with, but he liked my background, and I had great recommendations.

At that time, there were no postproduction departments in New York. The editor did it all: supervising the sound editing, ADR, foley, rerecording, labs, and prints.

BREAKING THE RULES

I was 34 when I got *Odds Against Tomorrow,* which was my first big feature. Bob Wise taught me that you have to follow a picture from the beginning all the way through to when they screw the lightbulbs into the marquee. I checked every theater and I picked every print that went out. In those days, you didn't print hundreds of prints on one roll; you did each individually.

A stylistic innovator, Allen began prelapping sound—beginning the sound-track ahead of the picture on a cut. In 1966, she edited Bonnie and Clyde. *Its unmatched cuts, fade-outs, and cut-ins have been greatly imitated.*

People in New York used to ask me, "How do you get into the business?" It's not just about getting in and cutting right away. I would always tell them to go to the theater. Anybody who's going to deal with dramatic material has to know what's a good performance and where a scene is. People coming out of TV and music videos do wonderful visual things, but a lot of them don't know scene structure or story. They have a whole different approach. With me, I guess my approach always had to do with acting and performance and story structure. Also, having come up in the business from the bottom, and working in many different departments, I learned all the phases of postproduction.

I have always told people there wasn't anything I learned along the way that didn't make me who I am as an editor.

My background gave me tremendous freedom in terms of sound and picture, and that's part of what I do. I can cut whole scenes without audio, and then my assistant can put the sound in, even with the overlaps, and very seldom is there any change. You can hear it and see it.

ACTOR'S LAB

When I first came to Hollywood, I worked evenings and weekends at Actor's Lab, which was an outgrowth of the Group Theatre in New York. I took directing classes and ran the sound on the plays. It was a wonderful little theater, and the actors were great. It was a tremendous learning experience. The Actor's Lab was eventually shut down by the blacklist.

In the beginning of my career I worked with editors who would let me come in and watch. I remember one guy who always said, "You have to start with the long shot, and then go to the medium shot, and then the close shot"—and of course that's not what you do at all. I don't cut that way, and the directors don't direct that way.

I also remember the first time a very good editor showed me how you stretch time with suspense. He would bring me in at night and show me. The generosity of people—you can't do it without help. Some people feel threatened, particularly if you are a rambunctious young woman who wants to learn. But people who feel threatened usually are people who aren't, well, very good at what they do.

WORKING WITH THE DIRECTOR

I had wonderful teachers: Robert Wise, Elia Kazan, Robert Rossen. You couldn't have had better teachers. I remember talking to Kazan once about a scene I was cutting, because he didn't look at anything until I had it all in one piece. I had one scene which I wanted to cut differently because the character had touched me so deeply, and I started telling Kazan about it. And he said, "Don't even tell me. It sounds wonderful. Show me." You have to have a director who's willing to trust you.

I always had directors who allowed me total freedom to do what I wanted. Confident people, like Arthur Penn and George Roy Hill, know what they're doing and don't have any problem with that. After all, they are in charge and able to change it.

Allen has always had close collaborations, not only with directors but with all the film professionals with whom she has worked.

Cinematographers are wonderful to work with. And writers, absolutely. I'm used to working with writers a lot. On *Bonnie and Clyde,* for instance, I was on the shoot in Dallas when we were doing the heavy-duty stuff, like the shoot-outs. It was a wild and wonderful experience. When we did the looping, Bob Towne would write stuff right at the Moviola for all kinds of voices and lines—in crowds (the scene with Buck's death), or off camera, if a line was needed.

I recently edited *John Q* for Nick Cassavetes. Nick is a terrific writer. If the format didn't work and we had to throw things out, he found a way of immediately writing new lines for the transitions. He went into my assistant's room and recorded the lines, we put them into the film, and later we replaced them with actors. I learned to work that way with Kazan on *America, America.*

Over the course of her career, Allen has seen major changes in both the styles and techniques of editing. The biggest change came with the emergence of the Avid, which computerized the editing process.

When I was starting out, film techniques were much more uniform. Then came the whole period where cameras got looser, sound was more flexible—everything changed. I went from film where you used to read your optical or magnetic tracks, which I cut in on the Moviola, to the Avid of today. All of them are nothing but tools.

The last picture I did on film the old way was the first *The Addams Family,* before I went to Warner Brothers as an executive.

LEARNING THE AVID LANGUAGE

I left Warner Brothers in order to cut *Wonder Boys.* It was tough for me to learn the Avid because I never learned to type. (I had thought that if I knew how to type, I'd be caught working in the stenographic pool— that's what happened to women at the end of the Depression.) So I had to learn the Avid language and think in a totally different way. It took me a long time to learn how to do through the Avid what I could do so fast on two Moviolas and a synchronizer. It drove me crazy in the beginning, but I had good and generous teachers, Stacey Clipp and Richie Marx, who had started out as my apprentice and assistant years before.

A Little Glossary of Editing ADR = Automated Dialogue Replacement, also known as looping. The actor rerecords words or lines in a studio after the scene or film has been shot. Avid = Digital editing workstation. Foley = Originally known as sync effects, usually body movements, such as footsteps or rustling clothes, are recorded later, in sync with the picture. Foley artists mimic the movements of actors on the screen to create the sounds. Magnetic track = Magnetic film and soundtrack stock with oxide on film base, used in double-system editorial to run synchronized sound with the visual image. Moviola = Upright editing machine for 35mm film and soundtrack editing, run by two pedals.

Allen has nurtured many young editors, passing along the favor granted her by her earliest mentors. She believes that people learning the craft need both "the umbrella and the freedom."

It's harder to teach with the Avid because the editor is much more separated from the assistant. Also, the people who know the mechanics of the Avid are very often people who came up through Avid, so they haven't had some of the other experience that the film people often had. They haven't had the exposure to the directors, who used to be more involved in every screening and look at the cuts, with the film assistants present for discussions as often as possible.

I always have a very open cutting room in terms of discussion. I always show everybody everything before I show it to the director. You have to have such an atmosphere so that when the assistants do start cutting, nobody feels threatened or insecure. As long as you give them the umbrella, you can develop a lot of good editors that way.

What It Takes to Make It

I always tell people to get into film any way they can. Don't start by being snobbish. Everything I learned in every part of the field—all of my experience in opticals, everything I picked up when I was doing commercials, and certainly my sound background—gave me the tools I needed for when I got to

work with a director like Bob Wise. I was always so excited about whatever chance I got, because in those days it was hard to break into the industry, especially as a woman.

It's a long, hard road. You have to want it. You have to find a way to meet people, which means you have to start ringing doorbells. You have to have enough bread when you come to a place like Hollywood to be able to support yourself when you're not working, because you won't work right away. And then you have to get in anywhere you can to start. It takes time and patience, but everything you gain gives you a little more confidence.

Studio Films Less Daring

Film editors were so snobbish about going into television in the beginning, which was kind of crazy, because it's all a part of the same craft, even though it's creative in a different way. That's all part of learning. And nowadays, HBO and Showtime are doing some of the best and most creative work. Meanwhile, the films have become much more about special effects, and less daring in terms of story and material. Studio films are made to get their money back fast, within the first weeks. Because they cost so much, they are aimed at mass audiences, often appealing to the younger audience category. The corporations are running the film studios, and it's all about the bottom line.

John Q (2002)   Wonder Boys (2000) **AAN, Best Film Editing   The Addams Family (1991)   Henry & June (1990)   Let It Ride (1989)   The Milagro Beanfield War (1988)   Off Beat (1986)   The Breakfast Club (1985)   Mike's Murder (1984)   Harry and Son (1984)   Reds (1981) **AAN, Best Film Editing   The Wiz (1978)   Slap Shot (1977)   The Missouri Breaks (1976)   Dog Day Afternoon (1975) **AAN, Best Film Editing   Night Moves (1975)   Serpico (1973)   Slaughterhouse Five (1972)   Little Big Man (1970)   Alice's Restaurant (1969)   Rachel, Rachel (1968)   Bonnie and Clyde (1967)   America, America (1963)   The Hustler (1961)   Odds Against Tomorrow (1959)   Terror from the Year 5000 (1958)
**AAN = Academy Award Nomination

MAYSIE HOY

EDITOR

Sometimes you leave the movie theater thinking, "Jeez, that character—he didn't feel right to me." It might have been because the transition of a character happened too early, too quickly, or it didn't happen at all. Sometimes editors are forced to cut out important moments in a character's life just to keep the movie within its promised length.

I ALWAYS LOVED TO TELL STORIES and studied to become an actor. I got my break when Robert Altman hired me for a part in *McCabe and Mrs. Miller*. But I was always intrigued by what happens behind the scenes and how a movie is put together. So I started to help out in several departments, from costume design to producing.

One day, I happened to stick my head into the editing room and saw the editor swamped in a sea of film, desperately searching for a missing trim. I asked if I could be of help.

Hoy stayed in that room, fascinated with the idea of being the tailor who sews all the pieces of the story together. The actors' performances, the dialogue, the cinematography, even the set design, background, and visual effects find their place with the guiding hand of the editor.

Although editing has many technical requirements, to me the process is a lot about intuition. When people ask me how I work, and how I cut a particular picture, I really don't know. It's like being a writer—you just become a source and open up to what's out there, and then the creativity happens.

Characters are everything to me. I get into the characters, I become the characters, which hopefully helps me make a truthful edit. That's the stuff that nobody taught me.

Before I sign to do a new project, I read the screenplay and ask myself, "Do I want to spend nine months with these characters?" I don't want to be stuck watching a bunch of whiners for almost a year.

When the shooting is finished, the editor slips into her darkened kingdom, only to emerge months later with circles under her eyes and a masterpiece in

her hands—or so many of us think. Not true. An editor is attached to a film at the very early stages, and she's on the set from the first day of shooting.

By the second day of shooting, I'm usually editing scenes and discussing them with the director. It helps the director, and it helps me—we both know early on where we are heading.

Hoy believes her ethnic background has helped in learning her craft.

In the Chinese language, many words have the same meaning. Subtle changes in the tone of your voice determine what the word means. Actors can say their lines in 50 different ways, and the look in their eyes adds 50 other meanings to what is said. Your job is to choose the perfect combination.

For those who are just starting out, school will give you the technical terminology. So when the editor says, "Give me the fill," "Give me the tracks," or "Give me that trim," you'll know what to do. You really need to go work for an editor. Be a P.A. (production assistant) or an intern or the runner in an editing room. That way you get to see how everything is done. It's a great place to get trained, and you will have fun doing it.

The ability to evaluate actors' performances is key. You have to learn about acting. That will also help you in terms of talking to your director. Be as well-rounded as you can be, and have as much knowledge of the techniques as you can get. Just don't become arrogant or come off as a know-it-all. Once again, it goes back to listening, and to listening to people's points of view without judging.

A Wrinkle in Time (2002, miniseries)   Christmas in the Clouds (2001)   The Warden (2001, pilot)   Freedom Song (2000, TV)   Crazy in Alabama (1999)   Life Tastes Good (1999)   What Dreams May Come (1998)   Love Jones (1997)   Freeway (1996)   Mrs. Munck (1996)   Smoke (1995)   The Joy Luck Club (1993)   Bank Robber (1993)   The Player (1992)   There Goes My Baby (1992)   Boris and Natasha (1992)

DEBBIE DENISE
VISUAL-EFFECTS PRODUCER

I help filmmakers tell their stories in ways that couldn't otherwise be done practically. There would be no way to train a little white mouse to talk and to steal everybody's hearts as in Stuart Little, *or to have children fly around on brooms in* Harry Potter. *It's really satisfying to help bring the filmmakers' imaginary world to the screen.*

I WORK VERY CLOSELY WITH THE PRODUCER OF THE FILM. We try to give the director the work he wants in the time frame and budget available. Almost anything is possible if you have unlimited time and money, but often that's not the case.

Debbie Denise was inspired to follow her dreams by the director of the broadcasting and film department at the University of Cincinnati. After moving to L.A., she wrote and produced promos at ABC, and then went north to Marin County, eventually working at Industrial Light & Magic. Currently, she is vice president of Sony Pictures Imageworks.

After I saw *Who Framed Roger Rabbit,* I thought, "I must work for these people at ILM." I just kept, figuratively, throwing myself up against their door. It took about a year and a half, but they finally agreed to take me on for a two-week assignment, which led into a five-year stay.

PUSHING THE ENVELOPE

I work closely with all the key department heads: the cinematographer, the production designer, sometimes the costumer and the makeup artist. The filmmakers sometimes need guidance as to how much we can push the envelope—what is possible, what has never been done but might be doable.

The length of each production varies, as does the size of the team. *Stuart Little* took two years, and we had about 150 people working on that movie. When you start projects that are cutting-edge, you don't really have a clear path in the beginning on how to create it. You just have to assemble the best team you can: software programmers, artists, your visual-effects supervisor, computer-graphics supervisor. You have to gauge your facility and invest in a brand-new digital pipeline for something that's never been done before. You need all those elements to pull it off.

When I was a digital coordinator for *Hook,* people hadn't yet realized how you could put opticals together with a computer. There was no software that helped you get from the Macintosh world to the film-resolution world. In *Death Becomes Her,* the digital-pipeline technology had developed further, but the director, Robert Zemeckis, wanted to do something nobody had ever seen before. We had to turn Meryl Streep's head all the way around and blend her real face into a CG (computer graphics) neck into her body, which was quite groundbreaking then.

You want to be able to transport the audience to an entirely different world, a world that is believable. With *Stuart Little,* people would tell me that, after seeing the first few minutes, they forgot he was a character, that he wasn't real.

In *Cast Away,* the island Tom Hanks was on was actually surrounded by a number of other islands. For the movie to really work on a deep, soulful level, he had to be entirely alone, with nothing around him. So we digitally removed all the other islands—as well as the wild goats on his island—to add to the feeling of isolation.

A believable digital human performance will probably be the biggest unsolved issue for a while in our industry. You can easily animate a digital human to take a fall or roll off of a mountain. But the performance is what's really tough. There's a certain amount of hesitation, even among the rest of the film world, to even get into it.

If you're an artist who wants to do visual effects, you can go to school, or you can work your way up from the bottom. Take a P.A. (production assistant) job or a technical assistant job. I really enjoy giving people a chance to work their way up. You feel like you've helped somebody in pursuing her dream and becoming a bona fide artist.

 Harry Potter and the Sorcerer's Stone (2001)   America's Sweethearts (2001)   Cast Away (2000)   What Lies Beneath (2000)   Snow Falling on Cedars (1999)   Stuart Little (1999) **AAN, Best Visual Effects   Contact (1997)   Michael (1996)   Sabrina (1995)   The American President (1995)   Forrest Gump (1994) *AA, Best Visual Effects   Death Becomes Her (1992) *AA, Best Visual Effects   Hook (1991) **AAN, Best Visual Effects   *AA = Academy Award   **AAN = Academy Award Nomination

RACHEL PORTMAN

COMPOSER

I love the use of a melody at the beginning of a film. You don't hear all of it; it's just suggested to you. As the story develops, you continue to hear bits of the theme here and there, and, finally, at the end, everything comes together, and it gives you a huge feeling of satisfaction. It may be an old-fashioned way to compose, but I think it works beautifully in film language.

Classically trained at Oxford University in England, Portman began her career composing music for theater. She spent many years in the U.K. trying to break into television by writing letters, sending tapes, and waiting for jobs to happen. In 1982, producer David Putnam hired her for her first job, on the made-for-British-TV film Experience Preferred . . . But Not Essential. *"He wrote me a very small check, but gave me a very big break," she recalls.*

I REALLY DEVELOPED MY CRAFT WORKING ON FILMS with a small- to medium-sized budget and orchestra size. Later on I started to compose for American movies, although I keep composing for European movies as well.

SOAKING IN THE FINISHED FILM

I step in when all of the elements of the film are close to completion. I start to extract from those elements the world in which the music should live. It's very important for me to spend a long time just soaking myself in the film. Because the music has to fit the scenes, I watch each scene again and again, to look at the pace of the film, and to see how long each scene is.

For me, composing is completely intuitive. The thing that gets me going is emotion. If there's something to say emotionally, then I'm interested. The second aspect is visual: the composer is painting a "soundscape" to match whatever the visual picture is. It's about balancing the film language that's being used and the emotion that's happening in the story.

You don't want to overdo a scene. If the scene is already sad, you don't want to add another sad layer to it. It needs to have varying layers so that when the audience hears the music, their feelings for the characters evolve.

I think brilliant composing can stand on its own. If you take the film away, buy the CD, and bring it home and listen to it, it has to work. Originality is important as well—something that's fresh, unexpected. When I watch and listen to a movie, I want to be surprised and dazzled.

Rachel Portman received Academy Award nominations for The Cider House Rules *and* Chocolat.

My main collaborator is the film's director. It's very much a two-way street, although the director is really the master whom I serve. It would be wrong of me to only do what I think is right, even though I have pretty strong ideas on what works or not. That being said, there have been times when I had to go back to the drawing board after I'd already done a large amount of work.

It happened with Lasse Hallström when working on *The Cider House Rules.* He is a wonderful director, very finely tuned, and has very good instincts about what is working. We had finished the movie and the score—we had one theme running through the entire film—and he said he had a feeling we may have got it wrong. He thought we needed to have a different theme for the beginning, the orphanage. I had to rethink 50 percent of the movie. That's very hard to do once you've gone deeply into a film score, and you've written and orchestrated it. I'm always happy to rewrite or think of new themes early on in the process, but it's harder once you've finished, because you feel like you've written a book.

I WANT TO BE STRETCHED

I choose my jobs on the basis of the director—whether it's someone whose work I really admire—and the script. I also ask myself, "Is it something I've done before?" It's got to be something new because I want to be stretched.

A couple of years ago, Jonathan Demme asked me to write the music for *Beloved,* from the book by Toni Morrison. During the interview, he said he did not want me to use any traditional instruments—no violins, no woodwinds, no pianos. I was so keen on working for him I agreed to do it. Then I embarked on this very long journey listening to music from all over the world, but mostly from Africa, because that's where we felt the roots of the music needed to be.

It was a huge exploration. I had the hardest, but most wonderful, time creating layers of score for him. It's the film score I'm most proud of, because I had to go on this journey and dig deeper. It was ironic in that

My favorite instrument is the clarinet because it's bittersweet. It's not romantic like a flute, or sad like an oboe can be. It's somewhere in the middle. You just can't tell exactly what it's trying to say, and I prefer that sort of slightly enigmatic coloring and shading.

he took away all the things I normally work with, all of my tools, so I had to create new ones.

A BALANCING ACT

I have three girls, ages one to five, the most wonderful beings ever. My biggest struggle now is to balance my life.

I work at home. I have to be incredibly disciplined about my working hours. I have to go through those painful days, weeks, when nothing is coming up, no ideas. But I have to make sure that I'm there from nine in the morning till six at night. If you put in those hours, eventually it comes. Which leaves the rest of my time for family, which is sacrosanct. I think I would be a horrid mom if I wasn't writing music. I'm a much happier, more balanced person when I'm doing a bit of both. I think having family and children inevitably changes the way you write and create. I don't know exactly how, but it's like you grow up, mature. The whole of my world is richer than it was before; I have a much greater emotional thing going on in my life than I used to, and it reflects in my writing.

Rachel Portman was the first female composer to receive an Academy Award, for her score for Emma.

If I had any advice for a woman breaking into composing, it would be to never give up trying if you're sure you want to do this. Don't focus on the obstacles. I've always thought of myself as a composer, not as a *female* composer. I've completely ignored the fact that I'm a woman working in a field where there are hardly any women.

The Truth About Charlie (2002)   Hart's War (2001)   Chocolat (2000) **AAN, Best Original Score   The Legend of Bagger Vance (2000)   Ratcatcher (2000)   The Cider House Rules (1999) **AAN, Best Original Score   Beloved (1998)   Marvin's Room (1996)   Emma (1996) *AA, Best Original Musical or Comedy Score   Palookaville (1996)   Smoke (1995)   War of the Buttons (1995)   Sirens (1994)   Only You (1994)   Ethan Frome (1993)   The Joy Luck Club (1993)   Benny & Joon (1993)   Used People (1992)   Where Angels Fear to Tread (1992)   Life Is Sweet (1991)   Experience Preferred . . . But Not Essential (1983, TV)   *AA = Academy Award   **AAN = Academy Award Nomination

MARILYN BERGMAN

LYRICIST

Why do singers gravitate to certain songs over and over again? Because they feel so good and effortless to sing.
I believe songs that are emotionally truthful will remain fresh over the years. Songs that observe the natural speech
rhythms and are married to original, yet inevitable melodies have the best chance of becoming standards.

I LITERALLY FELL INTO SONGWRITING. When I was going to college in New York, I fell down a flight of steps, breaking one shoulder and dislocating the other. I came to Los Angeles to recuperate at my parents' home. Bob Russell, a great songwriter whom I knew from New York, asked me what I was going to do while recuperating. He suggested I write songs. I told him that due to my injury, I couldn't possibly play the piano. "What about writing lyrics?" he asked. "You can dictate those into a tape recorder."

So I became a lyric writer. I often thought that if I had broken my legs, I would have been a composer. The first song I wrote was immediately recorded. It was an accident that gave purpose to the rest of my life.

I always loved the songs of the master songwriters, like Irving Berlin, George and Ira Gershwin, Cole Porter, Harold Arlen, Jerome Kern, Johnny Mercer. They were my models and inspiration. I studied their songs when I started my career, and I still find them inspiring and worth studying.

WHEN MORNING AND AFTERNOON MEET

I met my husband and collaborator, Alan Bergman, when he was writing songs in the morning with the same composer whom I was writing with in the afternoon. One day, the composer decided to introduce his morning lyric writer to his afternoon lyric writer, and the three of us decided to work together.

Alan and I have collaborated for close to 40 years, and our method has evolved over time. If Alan feels passionately about something, I respect his judgment enough to say, "Let's leave it your way for now and look at it again tomorrow," and vice versa. What usually happens is that it spurs us to look at a third way, which often is better.

Alan and Marilyn Bergman have been Academy Award nominees 16 times, and have received 3 Oscars.

A song in a film should have a function, not just exist to be a part of a soundtrack album. It should either underline a mood or add another level to what the characters are experienc-

ing. We always try to fly at a different altitude than the images. Take "The Windmills of Your Mind," written for *The Thomas Crown Affair.* Director Norman Jewison told us he wanted a song for the scene in which Steve McQueen is flying a glider, a song that would not reveal anything about the plot, but just underline the anxiety of the character.

PART OF THE FABRIC

Alan and I talked about the subtext of the scene. We talked about anxiety, about the feeling you have when you're waiting to fall asleep, and you try to turn your brain off but can't. Anxiety is circular, it feeds on itself. Michel Legrand wrote a melody, a long baroque ribbon, which felt perfect. The song wrote amazingly quickly. It was one of the few times in my life when I really understood what inspiration was.

I can't imagine ever robbing myself of the fun of being shown a film in a screening room and having something be born from the picture, something that grows out of it organically—as if you were always there, always part of that fabric, seamlessly.

Alan and Marilyn Bergman have collaborated with composers Michel Legrand, Marvin Hamlisch, Dave Grusin, Henry Mancini, André Previn, John Williams, Quincy Jones, and James Newton Howard, among others.

We prefer to have the music first. We feel that the piece ends up being stronger and more interesting in its structure and rhythmic patterns when the composer is unhampered by words. We always feel that there are words on the tips of the notes and we have to find them.

I grew up watching Fred Astaire and Ginger Rogers and the great MGM musicals. Unfortunately, the time we started writing coincided with the demise of those musicals, so we never got to write for Judy Garland or Gene Kelly or any other stars of those great musicals. I believe film musicals will come back, but in a different form. The young audiences who have grown up with music videos are accustomed to the combination of song and dramatic action and vignette and all the stuff that musicals are made of. It's not odd for them to see people sing and dance in a story context. You just have to find a way to make it work. Somebody will do it.

Lyrics are often confused with poetry, which they are not. Lyrics coexist in time with music. They can be poetic, but poetry is meant to be read, unlike lyrics, which are written for an instrument, the human voice. So the choice of words is words that sing, because first and foremost lyrics have to sing.

Sabrina (1995) **AAN, Best Song "*Moonlight*"   Shirley Valentine (1989) **AAN, Best Song "*The Girl Who Used to Be Me*"   Out of Africa (1985) "*The Music of Goodbye*"
Yentl (1983) *AA, Best Music, Original Song Score   Yentl (1983) "*Papa, Can You Hear Me?*" **AAN, Best Song   Yentl (1983) "*The Way He Makes Me Feel*" **AAN, Best Song
Best Friends (1982) **AAN, Best Song "*How Do You Keep the Music Playing?*"   Tootsie (1982) **AAN, Best Song "*It Might Be You*"   Yes, Giorgio (1982) **AAN, Best Song "*If We
Were in Love*"   The Promise (1979) **AAN, Best Song "*I'll Never Say Goodbye*"   Same Time, Next Year (1978) **AAN, Best Song "*The Last Time I Felt Like This*"   A Star Is Born
(1976) "I Believe In Love"   The Way We Were (1973) *AA, Best Song "The Way We Were"   Summer Wishes, Winter Dreams (1973) "*Summer Wishes, Winter Dreams*"   The Life
and Times of Judge Roy Bean (1972) **AAN, Best Song "*Marmalade, Molasses & Honey*"   Sometimes a Great Notion (1971) **AAN, Best Song "*All His Children*"   Summer of '42
(1971) "*The Summer Knows*"   Pieces of Dreams (1970) **AAN, Best Song "*Pieces of Dreams*"   The Happy Ending (1969) **AAN, Best Song "*What Are You Doing the Rest of Your
Life?*"   The Thomas Crown Affair (1968) *AA, Best Song "*The Windmills of Your Mind*"   In the Heat of the Night (1967) "*In the Heat of the Night*"   Television: Barbra Streisand:
The Concert (1995) Emmy, Best Original Song "*Ordinary Miracles*"   Brooklyn Bridge (1991) Emmy nomination, Best Song "*Just Over the Brooklyn Bridge*" (theme)   In the Heat
of the Night (1988) "*In the Heat of the Night*" (theme)   Sybil (1976) Emmy, Best Score   Alice (1976) "*There's a New Girl in Town*" (theme)   Queen of the Stardust Ballroom (1975)
Emmy, Best Score   Good Times (1974) "*Good Times*" (theme)   Maude (1972) "*And Then There's Maude*" (theme)   Brian's Song (1971) "*The Hands of Time*" (Brian's Song)
Theater: Ballroom (score, 1979)   *AA = Academy Award   **AAN = Academy Award Nomination   All lyric credits shared with Alan Bergman

TERI DORMAN

SOUND EDITOR

I never leave the theater—even if I don't like the movie—because I can always sit there and listen to it. I'm interested in the layered details of sound, and how sound can alter your perception of what the scene or the movie is all about. Sometimes sound creates the most compelling drama in a scene.

I WENT TO COLLEGE IN OHIO and studied broadcasting and entertainment, and moved to California to work in the movies. I started in the studio mailroom, and dropped off my resume on my mail runs to different departments, hoping to get a job. I was first hired in picture editing, and then I switched to sound, where I've been working for 26 years, the last years as a supervising dialogue editor.

A CIRCLE OF TALENTS

The sound department is truly a circle of talents, and the step-by-step process is very fascinating. Our work comes together on a mixing stage, where hundreds of levels and layers of sound are combined to create any one scene or atmosphere.

The process of sound begins when the film is shot. There is a production sound mixer and a boom operator on the set. They are recording all audio that is shot, taking notes and sound reports. They also record ambiances and backgrounds for set locations, and, occasionally, wild tracks of dialogue (dialogue without picture sync), in case there's a technical problem that occurs while shooting a particular scene.

After the picture editor has completed his or her edit, the material comes to postproduction sound. First, the sound-effects supervisor breaks down the script and decides what kinds of extra sounds may be needed. Then—since everything is digital these days—we take the sound from the original source, put it into computer drives, and start the process of cutting sound effects, dialogue, ADR (Automated Dialogue Replacement), foley (footsteps and movement tracks), the backgrounds, and the effects.

THE PROCESS OF DIALOGUE EDITING

My goal with dialogue editing is to create an atmosphere that is fluid, so that a scene that was shot over several days sounds like it's happening while you're watching it. The audience doesn't necessarily want to be bombarded by layers of loud sound; the balance of music, sound effects, and the quiet times is what creates the most interesting sound job.

Sometimes dialogue editing can be as simple as completing a syllable that cannot be heard in the audio track. Sometimes you need to rebuild a whole scene. For example, you are shooting a Western, and a plane flies over. The director might want to use that scene, although the audio track is unusable. I would then go through all the material that was shot and try to build an alternative track using an outtake that doesn't have that background, but that maintains the integrity of the acting, the directing, and the story. I would also have to provide a background track comparable with what's in the scene, or try to create the same on-set ambiance.

Sometimes it works beautifully, sometimes it doesn't. The alternative is to have an ADR editor step in and rerecord the actors' voices on a looping stage. That's rarely the best solution, though, because the sound in a room with a microphone is sterile and flat. Also, the rerecording usually takes place several months after the shooting has been completed, so the actors could be out of character, or their tone or their performance could be different.

Although it's a collaborative effort—I work with the picture editor, the director, and all of the sound department—my work itself is very solitary. It's a room with a machine and me, all of the production takes loaded into my machine. It's like building a giant puzzle.

CLOSEST TO THE DEADLINE

Unfortunately, sound is the last stage of the process before mixing. The movie has a release date, which means we are under a tremendous amount of pressure to meet that deadline, sometimes having to work terrible hours, seven days a week. The movie and its budget will determine how many people are hired to do any particular postproduction sound. *Pearl Harbor* had nine double reels of film—which is a very long film—so I ended up splitting the material between four dialogue editors and myself to be able to complete the movie on time.

I started out when film was all there was. Then everything changed to digital. I realized that I could learn the new technology and survive, or I could give it up to the kids who are coming out of college with only a knowledge of digital and the new technology. I went out and learned the system, which became *systems,* because there was no standard,

universally accepted piece of equipment. I ended up learning three or four systems. I feel I have more alternatives in editing because I know both the old and the new ways and can pull from either one when needed. I use things that I used in film every day, so it's not enough to just learn the latest system.

My advice to anybody wanting to work in sound would be to soak up as much knowledge as you can about the film industry—the way it used to be, the way it is, and the way it will become—because it's constantly changing and evolving. It's computerized, but it needs the operator who can draw on all of her past experience to come up with the best product.

I also think that in the very near future we'll have the capability of working at home and getting the information over the telephone line because it can be sent over wires. At the same time, I like to be involved in working with a team of people in the studio setting, so such opportunities will be a trade-off.

Spy Game (2001)   Pearl Harbor (2001)   Gone in 60 Seconds (2000)   Into the Arms of Strangers: The Kindertransport (2000)   The Thomas Crown Affair (1999)   Armageddon (1998) **AAN, Best Sound and Best Sound Effects Editing   Enemy of the State (1998)   Con Air (1997) **AAN, Best Sound   Red Corner (1997)   Sommersby (1993)   The Prince of Tides (1991)   Lethal Weapon 2 (1989) **AAN, Best Sound Effects Editing   Bird (1988) *AA, Best Sound   Nuts (1987)   Top Gun (1986) **AAN, Best Sound and Best Sound Effects Editing   Beverly Hills Cop (1984)   48HRS. (1982)   The Great Santini (1980)   The Deer Hunter (1978) *AA, Best Sound   King Kong (1976)   *AA = Academy Award   **AAN = Academy Award Nomination

It's challenging to come up with sound effects for things that don't exist—you have to use your imagination to figure out what else might sound like it. Or, when the actual sound doesn't work in the movie, you have to create a sound that's more subtle, more power-ful, or more detailed in order to get the effect you want.

Mary Pickford and screenwriter Frances Marion.

The Women Behind the Camera in Early Hollywood

BY CARI BEAUCHAMP

Women wouldn't be "given" the vote until 1920, yet years before that they were flourishing at every level of moviemaking as directors, producers, editors, and, most of all, writers. While writers' names often did not appear in the credits of the early films, from copyright records in the Library of Congress we know that almost half of all films written between 1912 and 1925 were penned by women.

MOVIES WERE AN IDEA ONE WEEK, before the cameras the next, and in the theaters within a month. With few people taking filmmaking seriously as a business, there were no paths to follow and no rules to break, and the doors were wide open to women.

Alice Guy was not only the first woman director, she was one of the very first film directors period, and is often credited with directing the first narrative film. She was a secretary to the Gaumonts in Paris in 1896, when they agreed to let her "play" with their cameras as long as her clerical duties didn't suffer. Her after-hours creations were so successful she was made the head of their quickly formed film-production company. She had literally given birth to the French film industry by the time she moved to America with her husband, the cameraman Herbert Blache. In 1910, she formed a film company in New Jersey, and supervised another several hundred films over the next four years.

Gene Gauntier began in pictures as an actress in 1906, but quickly moved to writing and directing. She claimed she could turn out three one-reel scenarios in a single day. Actress Helen Gardner formed her own production company in New York, in 1912, and made a dozen feature films under her own banner.

New York and New Jersey were the hub of activity in the early years. But as entrepreneurs and trustbusters dared to stand up to Thomas Edison and his consortium that held patents on movie cameras, few states were without some company with a camera at work. Nell Shipman traveled the country directing wildlife-adventure films, and there were dozens of other women who helped blaze the path. Margery Wilson directed several feature films as well, and wrote a half-dozen books. And Marion Wong, president of Mandarin Film Company, ran what was reported to be "the only Chinese producing concern" in America.

Southern California became an oasis—not only was the weather almost always perfect for outdoor filming, it was 3,000 miles away from Edison's trust and its vigilantes. It was a boomtown, where large houses and clusters of businesses were indiscriminately interspersed with lean-to refineries and thousands of oil wells, and then the occasional barn or deserted building on vacant land taken over by a roving band of moviemakers shooting "on the lot."

Los Angeles had been introduced to the "screen machine" in 1896, when the lights were dimmed at the Orpheum and the image of a life-sized Anna Belle Sun danced for a few precious moments, projected onto a large white sheet. The popularity of one-reelers shown between live vaudeville acts had grown so quickly that, by 1908, there were already 10,000 nickelodeons throughout the country desperate for product. As the demand for movies skyrocketed, the atmosphere was permeated with a sense of excitement. Anything was possible, and women flocked to Hollywood.

One of the first and most successful to direct in Los Angeles was a Blache protégée, Lois Weber. A pianist turned actress, Weber began to write and direct, and soon rose to the top using innovative camera angles, split screens, and detailed backgrounds and locations. With stories that stressed social significance and questioned prejudice, abortion, and society's priorities, Weber became the highest-paid female director in the country. Her film *Hypocrites*, featuring a reappearing naked woman dubbed "Miss Truth," packed the theaters and cemented her fame. "After seeing *Hypocrites*," said *Variety*, "you can't forget the name of Lois Weber."

Weber owned her own studio for several years and actively promoted other women. In turn, Weber was the most famous of a dozen women directors who found a booster in Carl Laemmle, the head of Universal. Cleo Madison starred in and directed dozens of films at Universal, as did Ida May Park, Ruth Ann Baldwin, Ruth Stonehouse, Lule Warrenton, and serial queen Grace Cunard. When Laemmle's "Universal City" opened in 1915, Lois Weber was named "Mayor."

Throughout the teens and early twenties, the pages of every new movie magazine announced scenario contests and advertised books like *How to Write for the Movies,* by a scenario writer for Chicago's Essanay studios, Louella O. Parsons. *Moving Picture* magazine's article

"A New Profession for Women" claimed women were natural writers, because they were used to writing letters and regarding paper as a confidant for their dreams and fantasies.

It would be as writers that women prospered for the longest period of time: the names of Frances Marion, Anita Loos, Bess Meredyth, Adela Rogers St. Johns, Zoe Akins, Lenore Coffee, June Mathis, and Catherine Turney laced the credits of films from 1914 into the 1950s. Jeanie MacPherson, another actress turned writer and then director, went on to lasting fame as the writer of many of Cecil B. DeMille's great epics. MacPherson and DeMille shared adjoining offices, and while many knew they enjoyed a decades-long affair, few confused their personal and professional lives; DeMille would have many mistresses but only a few screenwriters. Before writing *Gentlemen Prefer Blondes,* Anita Loos wrote the athletic comedies that brought Doug Fairbanks to stardom. Adela Rogers St. Johns wrote Westerns and social commentaries, Dorothy Davenport examined the evils of drug addiction and prostitution, Bess Meredyth wrote and directed *Tarzan* films and helped bring *Ben-Hur* to the screen, June Mathis discovered Rudolph Valentino for her adaptation of *The Four Horsemen of the Apocalypse,* and Jane Murfin wrote and produced *Stronghart* films, the popular forerunner of Rin Tin Tin. These women and dozens more like them wrote every conceivable genre of film. And no one was more in demand or more prolific from 1915 through the late 1930s than Frances Marion. For over two decades she was the world's highest-paid screenwriter—male or female—writing 200 produced films and winning two Oscars for her original stories *The Big House* and *The Champ.*

Marion's friendships were as legendary as her scripts. It was the vaudeville star Marie Dressler who first urged the San Francisco-born Marion to "jump into the movies," and the director Lois Weber took Marion under her wing in 1914. When Marion met the rising star Mary Pickford, the actress had played everything from Madame Butterfly to Cinderella. Pickford and Marion teamed up to create a character who stayed a child throughout *Poor Little Rich Girl,* and while the studio bosses balked at this little girl on the screen who reveled in mud fights, audiences clamored for more. From 1917 through 1919, Pickford and Marion perfected the girl-with-the-golden-curls persona in a dozen classics like *Pollyanna, The Little Princess,* and *M'Liss.* In the process, the women became the best of friends, and their friendship was to last a lifetime.

Adela Rogers St. Johns called Frances Marion "the senior all of us sophomores want to be," not only because of the respect Marion received within the film business, but because of her successful private life as well. Marion managed to raise two sons on her own after her husband, Fred Thomson, died suddenly of tetanus in 1928, and she kept her priorities clear. She joked that her huge Beverly Hills estate was "the house that bunk built" and confided to her best friends that, with the exception of Thomson, she had spent her life "searching for a man to look up to—without lying down."

When Marie Dressler's style of comedy was so out of fashion that she was facing dire poverty, Marion convinced Irving Thalberg, at MGM, to cast Dressler in a dramatic supporting role in a film Marion adapted for Greta Garbo, *Anna Christie.* Marion then wrote *Min and Bill* for Dressler, and the role won her the Best Actress Oscar. When Marion examined her own Oscar, she declared it "a perfect symbol of the picture business: a powerful, athletic body clutching a gleaming sword, but the half of his head, the part that held his brains, completely sliced off." Always practical, she used her Oscars for doorstops.

It is difficult to overstate the impact that the films these women made had on the hinterlands. Different mores, fashions, lifestyles, and countries were all seen for the very first time. Oh, you could read about these things in books if you sought them out, but suddenly there it all was, around the corner on the local big screen. Suffragettes marching in the newsreels built support for their cause; *A Girl's Folly* revealed both the tangible benefits and the emotional price of living the high life; the work of Margaret Sanger was promoted in *The Hand That Rocks the Cradle*—the list goes on and on. Their movies literally and figuratively opened up a whole new world to an entire generation.

Yet just as quickly as the opportunities for women to control their own creative product had opened, they began to close. When Cleo Madison could no longer find backers for her own films, she returned to acting in "minor roles in minor films." As early as 1919, Gene Gauntier became convinced the business had "passed her by" and moved to Sweden to write novels. Both Lois Weber and Alice Guy Blache suffered from the professional jealousies of their husbands, and both couples separated in the early twenties. Blache returned to France, and her efforts to direct in the late 1920s were rebuffed. Weber's "message films" left the Jazz Age audiences cold; while she attempted several "comebacks" during the twenties, she was managing an apartment building in Fullerton, California when she died, in 1939. "The premier woman director of the screen and author and producer of the biggest money-making features in the history of the film business" only two decades before, she warranted only a few lines of an obituary in *Variety*.

The advent of talking pictures in the late twenties demanded a huge influx of capital, so Hollywood turned to Wall Street. The hundreds of production companies that had flourished at the beginning of the decade fell victim to consolidations, mergers, and bankruptcies, reducing the number of profitable studios to only a handful by 1933. New layers of bureaucracy were added, jobs were tightly delineated, and with production and distribution controlled by only a few, women were pushed aside. Moviemaking was now big business.

A precious few of the women survived in the business into the late thirties, compromising along the way to the point where, Frances Marion said, "screenwriting became like writing on the sand with the wind blowing." Just as Rosie the Riveter was sent home after World War II, the women of Hollywood were no longer welcome in jobs men now wanted. A handful of women would continue to work behind the camera, but directors like Dorothy Arzner and Ida Lupino were the rare exception to the rule.

Many of the films these women created have been lost forever, but archives, such as those at the Museum of Modern Art, Eastman House, UCLA, and the Library of Congress, and organizations, like the National Film Preservation Foundation and the Women's Film Preservation Project, are racing against time to preserve those that remain. And while the number of women working in Hollywood today does not touch that of the early years, it is on the upswing once again. Today's women have a rich history to inspire them and claim as their own.

Cari Beauchamp is the author of Without Lying Down: Frances Marion and Powerful Women of Early Hollywood *and is a Writers Guild Award Nominee for cowriting and producing the documentary of the same name.*

OPPOSITE: Screenwriter Sarah Y. Mason.
Courtesy of the Academy of Motion Picture Arts and Sciences.

WOMEN WORKING IN FILM TODAY

BY MARTHA M. LAUZEN, PH.D.

IT SEEMS IRONIC that a community known for its progressive ideology and liberal politics remains decidedly retro in its employment of women. As a recent campaign by the activist organizations The Guerrilla Girls and Alice Locas noted, a higher percentage of women work as U.S. senators than as Hollywood directors. However, amid the cacophony of mostly misguided media and industry voices, the simple message that women remain chronically and dramatically underrepresented in the film industry has been muted.

A review of the research monitoring women's progress in the film industry reveals modest improvement over the last 15 years, with some retrenchment in the last few years. In 1987, women comprised 8 percent of all executive producers, producers, directors, writers, cinematographers, and editors working on the top 100 (domestic) grossing films, increasing to 10 percent in 1992 and 15 percent in 1997. After a small increase to 17 percent in 1998, women's representation declined to 16 percent in 1999 and 15 percent in 2000.

By role, women fare best as producers and worst as cinematographers. In 2000, women represented 22 percent of producers, 17 percent of executive producers, 13 percent of writers and editors, 7 percent of directors, and 2 percent of cinematographers.

Expanding the discussion to include the top 250 grossing films, women fare only slightly better. In 2000, women comprised 17 percent of behind-the-scenes individuals, accounting for 24 percent of producers,

16 percent of executive producers, 14 percent of writers, 19 percent of editors, 11 percent of directors, and 2 percent of cinematographers.

Of the various explanations offered for women's underrepresentation, perhaps none is so frequently mentioned or strongly held as the belief that films made by women earn less at the box office than those made by men. However, repeated analysis of box-office grosses by gender reveal that films employing women in key behind-the-scenes roles earn as much as those employing men. Another explanation for women's underrepresentation rests on the well-worn stereotype that women don't hire other women. In fact, our annual studies have consistently found that women hire significantly greater percentages of women than do men. For example, in 2000, films helmed by women directors employed 146 percent more women in other key behind-the-scenes roles than films with male directors.

Industry reaction to these statistics has been surprising, disappointing, and reaffirming. Overall, the silence from the studios has been deafening (though, when confronted with the statistics, one executive remarked, "That can't be right."). Denial. It enables executives and members of the creative community to dismiss the still-dismal numbers of women working in the film industry, simultaneously maintaining the status quo and their comfort levels. If the numbers "can't be right," they necessarily can't be.

Similar remarks appear in annual special issues of *Variety* and *The Hollywood Reporter* showcasing women in film and the most powerful women in entertainment. While many women acknowledge their own and others' experiences with gender discrimination, more than a few women comment that "the gender thing" is history. Often stating that they've never personally experienced the glass ceiling, they suggest that gender is a "nonissue" for women. These remarks seem particularly curious, as they often appear opposite articles and charts featuring the latest employment statistics.

Most likely, these statements reflect personal strategies for coping with inequitable, yet politically sensitive employment issues. While it's possible that the women interviewed have escaped gender discrimination in their professional lives, it seems more likely that they are feigning ignorance as a survival strategy. Recognizing the potential consequences of appearing difficult or, worse yet, strident, these women choose to place themselves outside the collective problem. In so doing, they thrust the burden for change on future generations of filmmakers.

Perhaps the most disheartening reaction to the research has come from some tremendously talented and weathered women who've remarked, "Things will never change for women in this business." Noting that the stubborn old-boys' network has morphed into the young-boys' network, these women see little hope for progress in the near or distant future.

Considering these reactions, it's unlikely that significant and sustained improvement in women's employment will result from simple evolution. It seems even more remote that the impetus for change will come from the studios, networks, or larger power structure currently ruling Hollywood. Change will most likely result from coordinated and strategic efforts by women and men in the film community. In part, these efforts may require a certain measure of anonymity for their organizers to short-circuit threats intimating, "You'll never work in this town again."

Using public embarrassment as a tool for change, a pointed publicity campaign by the anonymous Guerrilla Girls and Alice Locas recently targeted the film industry in general and the less-than-stellar track records of specific studios. The campaign used stickers to communicate the members' dissatisfaction with the current status of women in film. Accompanied by the tag line, "These distributors don't know how to pick up women," one sticker noted that Fine Line, Dimension, USA Films, and Shooting Gallery failed to release any films directed

by women in 2000. Miramax, New Line, Artisan, Sony Screen Gems, and Paramount Classics each released only one film directed by a woman in that same year.

On another front, some individuals are quietly investigating more litigious alternatives. Following in the footsteps of class-action lawsuits filed by women technicians against CBS and by mature writers against the television industry, these women believe that the only way to effect meaningful change is through judicial mandate.

Another solution may arise from organized solidarity. A number of groups—including the women's committees at the guilds, Women in Film, and the newly formed 50/50—currently provide excellent support networks and services for women. However, these groups work separately, often pursuing varied agendas. If members of these organizations could throw their collective resources, talent, and energy behind a strategic campaign intended to target opinion leaders in the industry and media, the prospects of broadened opportunities for women would certainly increase.

In the year 2000 women represented:

22% of producers

17% of executive producers

13% of writers and editors

7% of directors

2% of cinematographers

We also need a deeper understanding of hiring practices. There's still so much we don't know. How does the typical career trajectory for a woman filmmaker compare to a man's? Do women filmmakers experience the same kind of mentoring as their male counterparts? What are the roadblocks to women's progress, and how do they differ for women directors, writers, producers, cinematographers, editors, and executives? Without answers to these questions, it will be difficult to identify and implement workable and effective solutions.

At their inspired best, films reveal possible worlds. As a major producer and distributor of global culture, the U.S. film industry can promote diversity as an important value, or reinforce the less progressive agenda of a privileged few. Films can present the world as it is—or as it can be.

Dr. Martha M. Lauzen is a professor at San Diego State University. She conducts annual studies of women working in the film and television industries.

Our warmest thanks to our coproducers who made this book possible

ACADEMY OF MOTION PICTURE ARTS AND SCIENCES, Beverly Hills, California

CALUMET PHOTOGRAPHIC, LOS ANGELES, Jonathan Kanarek

M-REAL CORPORATION, Paper Galerie Art

PARIS PHOTO LAB & IMAGING, LOS ANGELES, Alain Labbe, Arnaud Gregori, and Marcelo Torok, digital artist

WARNER BROTHERS STUDIO FACILITIES COSTUME DESIGN CENTER, Burbank, California

Thank you.

For your invaluable support of our efforts to spotlight the cinematic arts: Academy of Motion Picture Arts and Sciences;
Ellen Harrington, Leslie Unger, and Robert Smolkin.

For believing in this project, and for your priceless help during the past year: project coordinator Mark Brown.

For making our visual dreams come true with the layout of this book: graphic designer Steve Mortensen, Santa Clara, CA.

For your insightful essays of the pioneering women of yesterday and today: Cari Beauchamp and Martha M. Lauzen.

For helping me to keep my voice clear: editor Natalie Nichols in Los Angeles.

For believing this could be a book, senior acquisitions editor Bob Nirkind—and, for making it worth reading, editor Gabrielle Pecarsky—at Billboard Books.

For your passion for great photography: Alain Labbe, Arnaud Gregori, and digital artist Marcelo Torok at Paris Photo Lab & Imaging in Los Angeles.

For letting us shoot the photos with the equipment we needed: Jonathan Kanarek at Calumet Photographic in Los Angeles.

For providing us with a wide selection of wardrobe choices for each shoot: Warner Brothers Studio Facilities, Costume Design Center, Pat Welch and the wonderful staff.

Corporate brand manager Susanna Serlachius at M-Real Corporation, Finland.

For making the women even more beautiful: makeup artist Elizabeth Dahl in Los Angeles.

For your energy and persistence in searching for support: Linda Arroz and Kyrian Corona of MakeOver Media.

For protecting our work: Leslie Abell at Myman, Abell, Fineman, Greenspan & Light, LLP, Los Angeles.

Photo Credits

DEDE ALLEN:
makeup Elizabeth Dahl.

JOAN ALLEN:
hair and makeup Cathy Highland/Cloutier,
jewelry Cathy Carmendy.

ALLISON ANDERS:
hair and makeup Elizabeth Dahl,
wardrobe Warner Brothers Studio Facilities
Costume Design Center.

JANE ANDERSON:
hair and makeup Elizabeth Dahl,
wardrobe Warner Brothers Studio Facilities
Costume Design Center, art director Zee Tankus,
camera assistant Kimberly Grisco.

MARILYN BERGMAN:
hair and makeup herself.

ROSEMARY BRANDENBURG:
makeup Cinzia Zanetti, hair Paul Awh,
production coordinator Denise Flachbart.

RUTH CARTER:
hair, makeup, and wardrobe herself.

BONNIE CURTIS:
hair and makeup Elizabeth Dahl,
production coordinator Lee Clay.

DEBBIE DENISE:
hair and makeup Elizabeth Dahl,
wardrobe Warner Brothers Studio Facilities
Costume Design Center.

TERI DORMAN:
hair and makeup Elizabeth Dahl,
wardrobe Warner Brothers Studio Facilities
Costume Design Center.

JODIE FOSTER:
hair and makeup Lucienne Zammet, wardrobe
Warner Brothers Studio Facilities Costume Design
Center, production coordinator Erin O'Donnell.

TRISH GALLAHER GLENN:
makeup Valli O'Reilly.

MAYSIE HOY:
hair and makeup Elizabeth Dahl,
wardrobe Western Costume.

VICKY JENSON, LORNA COOK,
BRENDA CHAPMAN:
makeup Elizabeth Dahl, makeup assistant

All women's costumes by Warner Brothers Costume Design Center.

Lab and digital imaging by Paris Photo Lab, Los Angeles.

Camera gear by Calumet Photographic, Los Angeles.

In Los Angeles, hair and makeup by Elizabeth Dahl.

Monique Hahn, wardrobe Warner Brothers
Studio Facilities Costume Design Center.

AVY KAUFMAN:
hair and makeup Hildie Ginsberg.

KASI LEMMONS:
hair and makeup Elizabeth Dahl,
wardrobe Warner Brothers Studio Facilities
Costume Design Center.

BETSY MAGRUDER:
hair and makeup Elizabeth Dahl,
wardrobe Warner Brothers Studio Facilities
Costume Design Center.

KERRY LYN MCKISSICK:
hair and makeup Elizabeth Dahl.

FREIDA LEE MOCK:
hair and makeup Elizabeth Dahl.

VE NEILL:
hair and makeup Ve Neill, wardrobe
Ve Neill and Warner Brothers Studio Facilities
Costume Design Center.

JEANNINE OPPEWALL:
hair and makeup Cinzia Zanetti.

RACHEL PORTMAN:
hair and makeup Elizabeth Dahl,
wardrobe Warner Brothers Studio Facilities
Costume Design Center.

LISA RINZLER:
hair and makeup Hildie Ginsberg.

JANE ROSENTHAL:
hair and makeup Laurel Steinberg.

SUSAN SARANDON:
makeup Genevieve/Sally Harlor, hair Keith
Carpenter, studio 5th & Sunset, New York.

CHRISTY SUMNER:
hair and makeup Elizabeth Dahl,
wardrobe Warner Brothers Studio Facilities
Costume Design Center, special-effects crew
Joe Andreas, Robert Hutchins, T.J. Lewis,
Tom Seymour, J.D. Streett.

ROBIN SWICORD:
hair and makeup Elizabeth Dahl.

CHRISTINE VACHON:
makeup Hildie Ginsberg,
location 71 Clinton Fresh Food, New York.

ABOUT HELENA LUMME

Author and filmmaker Helena Lumme offers a fresh and unique vision of the film industry. A devoted chronicler of movie history, she looks beyond the public facade of her subjects and paints insightful, intimate portraits of the men and women who create films.

Lumme's lifelong love of movies began in her native Finland and continues to be illuminated through her work. Her boldly artful projects are created in collaboration with an award-winning design team, including noted international photographer Mika Manninen. Their partnership has resulted in several memorable, visually stunning presentations destined to become an important part of the American movie heritage.

In 1997, Lumme produced *Screenwriters: America's Storytellers in Portrait,* a touring exhibition and book featuring portraits of 50 leading screenwriters. The exhibition was displayed at the Cannes International Film Festival, the European Film Awards in Berlin, and the Academy of Motion Picture Arts and Sciences in Beverly Hills. "With her work, Ms. Lumme has indeed done a unique service not only to writers, but to American film history in general," noted Writers Guild of America president Daniel Petrie, Jr.

Encouraged by the enthusiasm for *Screenwriters,* Lumme embarked on another journey—to make the contributions of women filmmakers better known throughout the moviemaking world.

"Hollywood is rich with talented female filmmakers," she notes. "I wanted to let the audience and the industry know about these spectacular women and their achievements."

"When I studied film," she continues, "the books didn't tell anything about women's contributions. I wanted to change that and show women actively working in all parts of the industry: They write and direct, shoot, build sets and blow them up, compose music… and earn Oscars while doing it."

Lumme selected 30 accomplished craftswomen from the major areas of filmmaking to be portrayed in *Great Women of Film.* She wanted to document their stories, the steps they took to reach the top, and their advice to young filmmakers.

"I hope to encourage young women to go where too few have gone before—making movies—and fully exploit all the opportunities today's film industry offers," she says. Lumme's nonprofit organization, Women's Film & Art Foundation, raises funds to award scholarships to talented women pursuing film careers.

Lumme's work has been covered by such major national media as ABC News, the *Los Angeles Times,* and the *San Francisco Chronicle,* as well as numerous European newspapers and magazines. She lives in Los Angeles.

About Mika Manninen

Over the past decade, photographer Mika Manninen has garnered an international reputation for his warm and humorous portraits of musicians, filmmakers, writers, and other artists. His photographic work has appeared in top magazines and has graced the covers of numerous books and CDs in Europe and the United States. His keen eye, unique approach, and exceptional technical skills have also made Manninen a sought-after director and cinematographer for commercials and film.

"I get very attached emotionally to my work—even more so when working on something personal like this book. We pour a tremendous amount of work and love into these projects," says Manninen.

Lumme and Manninen work together like a film team, planning and codirecting everything. Photographing and interviewing *Great Women of Film* took the couple a year. "We wanted to give the reader interesting stories to look at, stories that would tell something about each woman. Whether it was playing a particular role—real or fantasy—or taking part in their favorite hobby."

Manninen calls Los Angeles home but stays busy shooting photographs and film around the globe, maintaining a travel schedule that keeps him on the road 180 days of the year.

Mika Manninen, Jodie Foster, and Helena Lumme

APPENDIX

ORGANIZATIONS, SCHOOLS, AND RESOURCES THAT CAN HELP YOU GET WHERE YOU WANT TO GO

The Web sites of many of these organizations are worth visiting—they provide useful information
and links for both working professionals and those who are curious about a particular field.

ORGANIZATIONS SUPPORTING WOMEN IN THE MOTION PICTURE AND TELEVISION INDUSTRIES

AMERICAN WOMEN IN RADIO AND TELEVISION (AWRT) is a national nonprofit organization dedicated to advancing women in the electronic media and related fields. Established in 1951, AWRT has local chapters throughout the United States that promote AWRT's mission: to advance the impact of women in the electronic media and allied fields by educating, advocating, and acting as a resource to their members and the industry. AWRT, 1595 Spring Hill Road, Suite 330, Vienna, VA 22182. Phone: (703) 506-3290. E-mail: info@awrt.org. Web site: http://www.awrt.org.

CINEWOMEN is a nonprofit organization of professionals in the entertainment industry whose purpose is to support the advancement of women and their career goals in a noncompetitive environment. CineWomen is dedicated to developing the number and range of opportunities available to women in the industry, fostering a strong, independent spirit, and creating outreach projects that benefit the larger community. CineWomen/Los Angeles, 9903 Santa Monica Boulevard, Suite 461, Beverly Hills, CA 90212. Phone: (310) 855-8720. E-mail: cinewomen@aol.com. CineWomen/New York, P.O. Box 1477 Cooper Station, New York, NY 10276. Phone: (212) 604-4264. E-mail: info@cinewomenny.org. Web site: http://www.cinewomen.org.

50/50 is an outgrowth of the 50/50 Women Filmmakers' Summit, which occurred in April 2000, hosted by Allison Anders. The mission of the group is to attain equality for women in film and television, and all media now known or hereafter devised, worldwide, in perpetuity. Its strategic goals are: to increase the number of women directors working in film, television, and other media; to build audiences for women-directed films; to increase awareness of women's contributions to film and television history; to create mentorship opportunities for women; and to develop a community that will increase employment opportunities for women in film and television. Web site: http://www.5050summit.com.

INTERNATIONAL ALLIANCE FOR WOMEN IN MUSIC is devoted to fulfilling the purposes of the three organizations it unites. Created on January 1, 1995, through the uniting of the International Congress on Women in Music, American Women Composers, and the International League of Women Composers, the International Alliance for Women in Music celebrates the contributions of all women musicians, past, present, and future. Web site: http://www.iawm.org.

REEL WOMEN is a nonprofit organization formed for the purposes of developing a permanent support system for women at all levels of experience in the film and video industries. It aids and directly promotes the education, networking, and mentoring of women filmmakers; provides an information and resource pool to include audition notices, employment referrals, and access to equipment; and provides a supportive atmosphere for the exchange of information, assistance, and ideas. Reel Women, P.O. Box 50573, Austin, TX 78763-0573. Phone: (512) 292-9008. E-mail: reelwmen@texas.net. Web site: http://www.reelwomen.org.

SISTERS IN CINEMA is a resource guide for and about African American women filmmakers. Web site: http://www.sistersincinema.com.

WOMEN IN ANIMATION is a professional nonprofit organization established in 1994 to foster the dignity, concerns, and advancement of women who are involved in any and all aspects of the art and industry of animation. Women In Animation, Inc., P.O. Box 17706, Encino, CA 91416. Phone: (818) 759-9596. E-mail: info@womeninanimation.org. Web site: http://www.womeninanimation.org.

WOMEN IN FILM/LOS ANGELES (WIF/LA) is a leading nonprofit professional organization in the global entertainment, communication, and media industries. Founded in 1973 in Los Angeles, WIF provides an extensive network of valuable contacts, educational programs, scholarships, film finishing funds and in-kind grants, community outreach, and advocacy and practical services that promote, nurture, and mentor women to achieve their highest potential. WIF/LA, 8857 West Olympic Boulevard, Suite 201, Beverly Hills, CA 90211. Phone: (310) 657-5144. Web site: http://www.wif.org.

WOMEN IN THE DIRECTOR'S CHAIR (WIDC) is a Chicago-based international media arts/activist center which exhibits, promotes, and educates about media made by women that express a diversity of cultures, experiences, and issues. WIDC also serves as a network where independent women media artists share ideas, skills, and opportunities. WIDC, 941 West Lawrence, #500, Chicago, IL 60640. Phone: (773) 907-0610. E-mail: widc@widc.org. Web site: http://www.widc.org.

WOMEN MAKE MOVIES (WMM) is the largest distributor of women's media in North America, and is a national nonprofit feminist media-arts organization whose multicultural programs provide resources for both users and producers of media by women. WMM was established in 1972 to address the underrepresentation and misrepresentation of women in the media. WMM, 462 Broadway, Suite 500, New York, NY 10013. Phone: (212) 925-0606. E-mail: info@wmm.com. Web site: http://www.wmm.com.

WOMENFILMS.COM's mission is to offer quality, original content and provide an online community for fans of women filmmakers worldwide. E-mail: info@womenfilms.com. Web site: http://www.womenfilms.com.

COLLEGE AND UNIVERSITY DEPARTMENTS AND PROGRAMS

THE ACADEMY OF ART COLLEGE offers B.F.A., M.F.A., and certificate programs in art and design. Academy of Art College, 79 New Montgomery Street, San Francisco, CA 94105. Phone: (800) 544-ARTS. E-mail: info@academyart.edu. Web site: http://www.academyart.edu.

BROOKLYN COLLEGE Department of Film is the only public undergraduate department of film production and film studies in the New York area, integrating both forms of study in all concentrations offered. Brooklyn College – CUNY, Department of Film, 2900 Bedford Avenue, 0314 Plaza Building, Brooklyn, NY 11210. Phone: (718) 951-5664. E-mail: film@brooklyn.cuny.edu. Web site: http://depthome.brooklyn.cuny.edu/film.

CALIFORNIA INSTITUTE OF THE ARTS (CalArts) has established a national and international reputation as a leader in the visual and performing arts. CalArts, 24700 McBean Parkway, Valencia, CA 91355. Phone: (661) 255-1050. Web site: http://www.calarts.edu.

CALIFORNIA STATE UNIVERSITY, LONG BEACH (CSULB) Film and Electronic Arts program is an innovative academic program that emphasizes both professional education and liberal arts through both media theory and practice. CSULB, 1250 Bellflower Boulevard, Long Beach, CA 90840-2004. Phone: (562) 985-4364. Web site: http://www.csulb.edu.

COLLEGE OF SANTA FE is committed to developing a creative environment where students can produce work that challenges the prevailing political, cultural, and aesthetic conventions. College of Santa Fe, Moving Image Arts, 1600 St. Michael's Drive, Santa Fe, NM 87505. Phone: (800) 456-2673 ext. 6400 or (505) 473-6400. E-mail: mov@csf.edu. Web site: http://www.csf.edu/mov.

COLUMBIA UNIVERSITY SCHOOL OF THE ARTS combines history, theory, and criticism of film with directing, writing, and producing to provide students with a deep understanding of the principles and practice of cinematic storytelling. Columbia University, 305 Dodge Hall, Mail Code 1808, 2960 Broadway, New York, NY 10027. Phone: (212) 854-2875. E-mail: admissions-arts@columbia. Web site: http://www.columbia.edu.

DEANZA COLLEGE's Film/Television department offers several courses of study in live action and animation. DeAnza College, 21250 Stevens Creek Boulevard, Cupertino, CA 95014. Phone: (408) 864-5678. Web site: http://www.deanza.fhda.edu.

EMERSON COLLEGE is the nation's only four-year college devoted exclusively to the study of communication and performing arts. Emerson College, 120 Boylston Street, Boston, MA 02116-4624. Phone: (617) 824-8500. Web site: http://www.emerson.edu.

FLORIDA STATE UNIVERSITY FILM SCHOOL operates its main studios in Tallahassee and its music-recording stage and back-lot property in Quincy, Florida. Taken together, these facilities are among the largest and best equipped in the world devoted wholly to film education. It is the only school in America that pays for all of its students' production expenses, including their thesis films. All together, more than 150 complete sound films are made by students each year, of which 10-12 are thesis films. Florida State University Film School, University Center 3100A, Tallahassee, FL 32306-2350. Phone: (850) 644-7728. Web site: http://www.filmschool.fsu.edu.

FRANKLIN & MARSHALL COLLEGE of Theatre, Dance, and Film is dedicated to the integration of theory and practice, and devoted to providing all students—whatever their major—with interdisciplinary opportunities across the spectrum of the performing arts. Franklin & Marshall College, P.O. Box 3003, Lancaster, PA 17604-3003. Phone: (717) 291-3911. Web site: http://www.fandm.edu.

JOHNS HOPKINS UNIVERSITY Film and Media Studies Program incorporates courses in history, criticism, theory, and screenwriting with courses in film, television, and multimedia production. John Hopkins University, Gilman 146, 3400 North Charles Street, Baltimore, MD 21218. Phone: (410) 516-4313. E-mail: english@jhu.edu. Web site: http://www.jhu.edu/~english/film_media/index.html.

LOS ANGELES CITY COLLEGE (LACC) Department of Cinema and Television provides basic and advanced production courses. LACC, Cinema-Television Department, Communications Center, 855 North Vermont Avenue, Los Angeles, CA 90029. Phone: (323) 953-4545. E-mail: obernvg@E-mail.lacc.cc.ca.us. Web site: http://www.citywww.lacc.cc.ca.us.

MIDDLEBURY COLLEGE Film and Video Program emphasizes a broad liberal-arts approach that combines training in hands-on skills, such as video production and screenwriting, with studies of film/video history, criticism, and aesthetics. Middlebury College, Film/Video Studies, Wright Theatre, Middlebury, VT 05753. Phone: (802) 443-3190. Web site: http://www.middlebury.edu.

MOUNT HOLYOKE Film Studies Program introduces students to the academic study of film from a variety of critical and disciplinary perspectives. Courses combine cultural, historical, formal, and theoretical analysis of films from a range of world cinematic traditions. Mount Holyoke College, Film Studies Program, Art Building, South Hadley, MA 01075. Phone: (413) 538-2200. Web site: http://www.mtholyoke.edu.

NORTH CAROLINA SCHOOL OF THE ARTS'S (NCSA) primary purpose is the professional training, as distinguished from liberal-arts instruction, of talented students in the fields of music, drama, dance, and the allied performing arts, at both high school and college levels of instruction, with emphasis placed upon performance rather than academic studies of the arts. NCSA, 1533 South Main Street, Winston-Salem, NC 27127-2188. Phone: (336) 770-3399. Web site: http://www.ncarts.edu.

RINGLING SCHOOL OF ART AND DESIGN is a four-year college of visual arts and design. Students pursue a B.F.A. in one of six majors: computer animation, fine arts, graphic and interactive communication, illustration, interior design, and photography and digital imaging. Ringling School of Art and Design, 2700 North Tamiami Trail, Sarasota, FL 34234-5895. Phone: (800) 255-7695 or (941) 351-5100. Web site: http://www.rsad.edu.

SAN DIEGO STATE UNIVERSITY College of Professional Studies and Fine Arts Program focuses on skills required for careers as producers, directors, art directors, production assistants, and writers, as well as for emerging careers in new-media production. San Diego State University, 5500 Campanile Drive, San Diego, CA 92182-4561. Phone: (619) 594-5450. E-mail: socdesk@mail.sdsu.edu. Web site: http://www rohan.sdsu.edu/dept/schlcomm.

SAN FRANCISCO STATE UNIVERSITY (SFSU) Cinema Department was founded amid the political activism and artistic experimentation of the 1960s. Today, as then, the Cinema Department is committed to a curriculum that recognizes cinema to be an independent, powerful, and unique medium in the world. Cinema programs combine theory and practice; students are encouraged to engage in scholarship and to pursue production in all forms of cinematic expression. SFSU Cinema Department Fine Arts Building, Room 245, 1600 Holloway Avenue, San Francisco, CA 94132-4157. Phone: (415) 338-1629. E-mail: cinedept@sfsu.edu. Web site: http://www.cinema.sfsu.edu.

UNIVERSITY OF CALIFORNIA LOS ANGELES (UCLA) School of Theater, Film, Television and Digital Media offers programs in the history and theory as well as the creative and technical aspects of the moving image. UCLA/TFT, 405 Hilgard Avenue, Box 951361, Los Angeles, CA 90095-1361. Phone: (310) 825-4321. Web site: http://www.tft.ucla.edu.

UNIVERSITY OF CALIFORNIA BERKELEY Film Studies Program offers an undergraduate major in film. University of California, Program in Film Studies, 7408 Dwinelle Hall # 2670, Berkeley, CA 94720-2670. Phone: (510) 642-1415. Web site: http://cinemaspace.berkeley.edu.

UNIVERSITY OF KANSAS Department of Theatre and Film offers a variety of degrees in several fields of film and theater studies. University of Kansas, Department of Theatre and Film, 356 Murphy Hall, Lawrence, KS 66045. Phone: (913) 864-3511. Web site: http://www.ku.edu.

UNIVERSITY OF OKLAHOMA Film and Video Studies program is designed to give students a broad understanding of the role of film and video in modern society. University of Oklahoma, 640 Parrington Oval, Norman, OK 73019-3050. Phone (405) 325-3020. E-mail: fvs@ou.edu. Web site: http://www.ou.edu/fvs.

UNIVERSITY OF SOUTHERN MAINE Media Studies offers programs in media writing, media criticism, and multimedia production and design. University of Southern Maine, Media Studies, 19 Chamberlain Avenue, Portland, ME 04103. Phone: (207) 780-5972. Web site: http://www.usm.maine.edu.

UNIVERSITY OF UTAH College of Fine Arts prepares students for employment in the motion picture industry or entry into the teaching profession. Students are required to do significant production work in film, video, and screenwriting. In addition to course work in production, students undertake substantial work in film history, theory, and criticism. University of Utah, Division of Film Studies, 375 S 1530 E, Room 257B, Salt Lake City, UT 84112-0380. Phone: (801) 581-5127. Web site: http://www.film.utah.edu.

GRADUATE PROGRAMS

AMERICAN FILM INSTITUTE (AFI) is the nation's preeminent arts organization dedicated to advancing and preserving the art of the moving image. Since 1967, AFI has served as America's voice for film, television, video, and the digital arts, with innovative programs in education, training, exhibition, preservation, and new technology. AFI, 2021 North Western Avenue, Los Angeles, CA 90027. Phone: (323) 856-7600. E-mail: info@afionline.org. Web site: http://www.AFIonline.org. The AFI Directing Workshop for Women (DWW) has been a major force in training women in narrative filmmaking since 1974. More than 150 women have been given the opportunity to participate in this unique training program for tomorrow's directors. The DWW is designed specifically for women who are working in the arts and are ready to seriously pursue narrative directing. AFI Directing Workshop for Women, 2021 North Western Avenue, Los Angeles, CA 90027. Phone: (323) 856-7628.

CHAPMAN UNIVERSITY SCHOOL OF FILM AND TELEVISION Chapman University, School of Film and Television, Cecil B. DeMille Hall, 333 North Glassell Street, Orange, CA 92866. Phone: (714) 997-6765. E-mail: ftvinfo@chapman.edu. Web site: http://www.chapman.edu.

NEW YORK UNIVERSITY-TISCH SCHOOL OF THE ARTS New York University-Tisch School of the Arts, 70 Washington Square South, New York, NY 10012. Phone: (212) 998-1212. Web site: http://www.nyu.edu/tisch/filmtv.

OHIO UNIVERSITY SCHOOL OF FILM offers two graduate-degree programs, the Master of Fine Arts (M.F.A.) and the Master of Arts (M.A.), designed to allow the entrance of talented students with no formal film training who have demonstrated extensive experience in another medium or academic discipline. While prior achievement in filmmaking, video, or film scholarship is not necessary, acceptance to graduate study in the school requires a major commitment to these areas of study. Ohio University School of Film, Lindley Hall 378, Athens, OH 45701. Phone: (740) 593-1323. E-mail: filmdept@www.ohiou.edu. Web site: http://www.ohiou.edu.

SHERIDAN COLLEGE Sheridan Center of Animation and Emerging Technologies offers advanced studies in animation, television, and film. Sheridan Center for Animation and Emerging Technologies, 1430 Trafalgar Road, Oakville, ON L6H2L1, Canada. Phone: (905) 845 9430. E-mail: http://www.sheridanc.on.ca.

TEMPLE UNIVERSITY's M.F.A. program in Film and Media Arts is the country's foremost program in alternative film and video, training filmmakers, videomakers, screenwriters, and media artists who seek to challenge the current practices of Hollywood and commercial television. The department also offers a Bachelor of Arts program in media production and theory, focusing on the development of creative and technical skills in film, video, audio, multimedia, computers, and new technologies, and the theoretical understanding of media and culture. Temple University, Department of Film and Media Arts, 9 Annenberg Hall, Philadelphia, PA 19122. Phone: (215) 204-3859. E-mail: fmahelp@temple.edu. Web site: http://www.temple.edu.

UNIVERSITY OF ALABAMA Telecommunication and Film Department University of Alabama, Box 870152 Tuscaloosa, AL 35487-0152. Phone: (205) 348-6350. Web site: http://www.tcf.ua.edu.

UNIVERSITY OF IOWA Department of Cinema and Comparative Literature provides intensive work in literature, film and audiovisual study, film and video production, literary theory, and critical methods. University of Iowa, 425 English-Philosophy Building, Iowa City, IA 52242. Phone: (319) 335-0330. E-mail: cinema-complit@uiowa.edu. Web site: http://www.uiowa.edu.

UNIVERSITY OF NORTH TEXAS Department of Radio, Television, and Film. University of North Texas, Department of Radio, Television, and Film, General Academic Building, Room 435, P.O. Box 310598, Denton, TX 76203-0598. Phone: (940) 565-2537. Web site: http://www.rtvf.unt.edu.

UNIVERSITY OF SOUTHERN CALIFORNIA School of Cinema-Television. USC School of Cinema-Television, University Park, Los Angeles, CA 90089-2211. Phone: (213) 740-2804. Web site: http://www.usc.edu.

UNIVERSITY OF TEXAS AT AUSTIN Department of Radio, Television and Film. University of Texas at Austin, Department of Radio, Television and Film, CMA 6.118, Austin, TX 78712-1091. Phone: (512) 471-4071 or 471-3532. Web site: http://www.utexas.edu.

UNIVERSITY OF WISCONSIN AT MILWAUKEE School of the Arts. UW-Milwaukee Director of Graduate Studies, Film Department, P.O. Box 413, Milwaukee, WI 53201-0413. Phone: (414) 229-6015. Web site: http://www.uwm.edu.

SCHOOLS AND WORKSHOPS

CINEMA TRAINING CENTER is a vocational trade film school where working professionals train future pros. Cinema Training Center, 11335 Magnolia Boulevard, North Hollywood, CA 91601. Phone: (818) 623-0459. E-mail: question@cinematrainingcenter.com. Web site: http://www.cinematrainingcenter.com.

COLUMBIA COLLEGE - HOLLYWOOD (CCH) has been training students for technical and creative roles in the entertainment industry since 1952. CCH offers Bachelor of Arts degrees in cinema and in television/video production. CCH, 18618 Oxnard Street, Tarzana, CA 91356. Phone: (800) 785-0585 or (818) 345-8414. Web site: http://www.columbiacollege.edu.

DH INSTITUTE OF MEDIA ARTS'S (DHIMA) mission is to help its students become digital artists and excel in real-world production environments. DHIMA, 1315 Third Street, Suite 300, Santa Monica, CA 90401. Phone: (310) 899-9377. E-mail: info@dhima.com. Web site: http://www.dhima.com.

EUROPEAN FILM COLLEGE is the only pan-European school devoted to the art and craft of film. European Film College, Carl Th. Dreyers Vej 1, DK-8400 Ebeltoft, Denmark. Phone: 45 86 34 0055. E-mail: administration@efc.dk.

HOLLYWOOD FILM SCHOOL offers the training and exposure required for such jobs as screenwriting, computer special effects, mechanical special effects, and production assistants. Hollywood Film School, Townsgate Road, Suite K, Westlake Village, CA 91361. Phone: (805) 496-9716. E-mail: info@hfsti.com. Web site: http://www.hollywoodfilmschool.com.

LONDON INTERNATIONAL FILM SCHOOL offers a two-year, full-time diploma course in the art and technique of filmmaking. London International Film School, 24 Shelton Street, London WC2H 9UB, U.K. Phone: 44 (0)20 7836 9642. Web site: http://www.lifs.org.uk.

LOS ANGELES FILM SCHOOL Los Angeles Film School, 6363 Sunset Boulevard, Suite 400, Hollywood, CA 90028. Phone: (323) 860-0789. Web site: http://www.lafilm.com.

MAINE PHOTOGRAPHIC FILM AND TELEVISION WORKSHOPS is a leading workshop center for the world's imagemakers, photographers, journalists, filmmakers, writers, and artists. The Workshops, P.O. Box 200, 2 Central Street, Rockport, ME 04856. Phone: (877) 577-7700 or (207) 236-8581. E-mail: info@theworkshops.com. Web site: http://www.meworkshops.com.

MOTION PICTURE INSTITUTE OF MICHIGAN is a hands-on film trade school offering a one-year program concentrating on independent feature film and commercial film production. Motion Picture Institute of Michigan, 295 Elm, Suite 4, Birmingham, MI 48009. Phone: (248) 723-5735. E-mail: info@mpifilm.com. Web site: http://www.mpifilm.com.

NATIONAL FILM SCHOOL OF DENMARK is aimed at professional film/television/video production. National Film School of Denmark , Theodor Christensens Plads 1, 1437 Copenhagen K, Denmark, Phone: 45 32 68 64 00. Web site: http://www.filmskolen.dk

NEW YORK FILM ACADEMY (NYFA) offers workshops providing students with intensive, hands-on experience. NYFA, 100 East 17th Street, New York, NY 10003. Phone: (212) 674-4300. Web site: http://www.nyfa.com

VANCOUVER FILM SCHOOL (VFS) programs focus on industries that use moving images, graphics, sound, and text as fundamental components for communicating information and story. VFS programs, as a matter of design, regularly and continually evolve in response to current industry methodology, technology, and need. Vancouver Film School, 198 West Hastings Street, Vancouver, BC V6B 1H2, Canada. Phone: (604) 685-5808. E-mail: registrar@vfs.com. Web site: http://www.vfs.com

GUILDS AND UNIONS

ACTORS' EQUITY ASSOCIATION (AEA) is the labor union representing over 40,000 American actors and stage managers working in professional theater. Equity negotiates minimum wages and working conditions, administers contracts, and enforces the provisions of various agreements with theatrical employers across the country. AEA, National Headquarters, 165 West 46th Street, 15th Floor, New York, NY 10036. Phone: (212) 869-8530. Web site: http://www.actorsequity.org.

ALLIANCE OF CANADIAN CINEMA, TELEVISION AND RADIO ARTISTS (ACTRA) is a national organization of professional performers working in the recorded media in Canada. ACTRA has ten branches across Canada. ACTRA, 625 Church Street, Toronto, Ontario, Canada M4Y 2G1. Phone: (800) 387-3516 or (416) 489-1311. Web site: http://www.actra.com.

AMERICAN FEDERATION OF TELEVISION AND RADIO ARTISTS (AFTRA) is a national labor union affiliated with the AFL-CIO. Its headquarters is in New York, with 36 local offices throughout the country. AFTRA represents its 80,000 members in four major areas: news and broadcasting; entertainment programming; the recording business; and commercials and nonbroadcast, industrial, educational media. Actors, announcers, news broadcasters, singers (including royalty artists and background singers), dancers, sportscasters, disc jockeys, and talk show hosts comprise AFTRA's membership. AFTRA, National Office - New York, 260 Madison Avenue, New York, NY 10016-2402. Phone: (212) 532-0800. National Office - Los Angeles, 5757 Wilshire Boulevard, 9th Floor, Los Angeles, CA 90036-3689. Phone: (323) 634-8100. Web site: http://www.aftra.org.

DIRECTOR'S GUILD OF AMERICA (DGA) represents members who work in theatrical, industrial, educational, and documentary films, as well as live, filmed, and taped television programs, radio, videos, and commercials. The Women's Steering Committee within DGA specializes in advancing women's employment in the industry. DGA and Women's Steering Committee, 7920 Sunset Boulevard, Los Angeles, CA 90046. Phone: (310) 289-2000 or (800) 421-4173. Web site: http://www.dga.org.

INTERNATIONAL ALLIANCE OF THEATRICAL STAGE EMPLOYEES (IATSE) is the labor union that represents technicians, artisans, and craftspersons in the entertainment industry, including live theater, film, and television production. IATSE General Office, 1515 Broadway, Suite 601, New York, NY 10036. Phone: (212) 730-1770. Web site: http://www.iatse.lm.com.

INTERNATIONAL CINEMATOGRAPHERS GUILD (IATSE, Local 600) promotes the talents and defends the financial interests and artistic rights of camera professionals from across the United States and around the world. Its nearly 5,000 members include directors of photography, camera operators, assistants, still photographers, animators, and visual-effects specialists. International Cinematographer's Guild, 7715 Sunset Boulevard, Suite 300, Hollywood, CA 90046. Phone: (323) 876-0160. Web site: http://www.cameraguild.com.

MOTION PICTURE EDITORS GUILD (IATSE, Local 776) is a labor union representing picture, sound, and music editors, sound mixers, and technicians in motion picture and television productions. The Motion Picture Editors Guild, 7715 Sunset Boulevard, Suite 200, Hollywood, CA 90046. Phone: (800) 705-8700 or (323) 876-4770. Web site: http://www.editorsguild.com.

THE PRODUCERS GUILD OF AMERICA represents, protects, and promotes the interests of all members of the producing team. The Producers Guild of America, 6363 Sunset Boulevard, 9th Floor Hollywood, CA 90028. Phone: (323) 960-2590. Web site: http://www.producersguild.org.

SCREEN ACTORS GUILD (SAG) represents its 86,000 members through negotiation and enforcement of collective bargaining agreements that establish equitable levels of compensation, benefits, and working conditions for performers; through the collection of compensation for exploitation of their recorded performances and protection against unauthorized use; and the preservation and expansion of work opportunities. SAG has a women's committee dedicated to women's issues. SAG National Office, 5757 Wilshire Boulevard, Los Angeles, CA 90036-3600. Phone: (323) 954-1600. Web site: http://www.sag.com.

WRITERS GUILD OF AMERICA (WGA) represents over 8,000 writers in the motion picture, broadcast, cable, and new technologies industries. WGA has appointed a women's committee that advances women's employment in the industry. WGA/West , 7000 West Third Street, Los Angeles, CA 90048. Phone: (323) 951-4000. Web site: http://www.wga.org. WGA/East, 555 West 57th Street, Suite 1230, New York, NY 10019. Phone: (212) 767-7800. Web site: http://www.wgaeast.org.

ADDITIONAL ORGANIZATIONS AND RESOURCES

AMERICAN CINEMA EDITORS (ACE) is an honorary society made up of editors deemed to be outstanding in their field. ACE sponsors an annual student editing competition and an internship program for college graduates seeking a career in editing. ACE, 100 Universal City Plaza, Building 2282, Room 234, Universal City, CA 91608. Phone: (818) 777-2900. Web site: http://www.ace-filmeditors.org.

AMERICAN SCREENWRITERS ASSOCIATION™ is committed to the international support and advancement of all screenwriters, welcoming interested individuals from around the world who are pursuing the writing of documentaries, educational films, feature films, television, and large-screen format films. American Screenwriters Association, 269 South Beverly Drive, Suite 2600, Beverly Hills, CA 90212-3807. E-mail: asa@asascreenwriters.com. Web site: http://www.asascreenwriters.com.

AMERICAN SOCIETY OF CINEMATOGRAPHERS (ASC) membership is awarded for outstanding achievements in cinematography. Their magazine, *American Cinematographer,* is the leading authority in the field, and their Web site serves the cinematographic community. ASC, 784 North Orange Drive, Hollywood, CA 90028. Phone: (800) 448-0145 or (323) 969-4333. Web site: http://www.cinematographer.com.

AMERICAN SOCIETY OF COMPOSERS, AUTHORS AND PUBLISHERS (ASCAP) is a membership association of over 120,000 composers, songwriters, lyricists, and music publishers. ASCAP's function is to protect the rights of its members by licensing and paying royalties for the public performances of their copyrighted works. ASCAP – New York, One Lincoln Plaza, New York, NY 10023. Phone: (212) 621-6000. E-mail: info@ascap.com. Web site: http://www.ascap.com. ASCAP – Los Angeles, 7920 W. Sunset Boulevard, 3rd Floor, Los Angeles, CA 90046. Phone: (323) 883-1000.

BLACK HOLLYWOOD EDUCATION AND RESOURCE CENTER is a nonprofit organization designed to advocate, educate, research, develop, and preserve the history and the future of blacks in the film and television industries. The BHERC strives to highlight the important roles that blacks have played, and continue to play, in film and television. To that end, the BHERC celebrates and promotes black history and culture through a series of annual film festivals that recognize black film and television pioneers. Black Hollywood Education and Resource Center, 1888 Century Park East, Suite 1900, Los Angeles, CA 90067-2199. Phone: (310) 284-3170. 24-hour hotline: (323) 957-4747. E-mail: bherc@bherc.org. Web site: http://www.bherc.org.

FILM ARTS FOUNDATION provides comprehensive training, equipment, information, consultations, and exhibition opportunities to independent filmmakers. With more than 3,400 members working in film, video, and multimedia, it is the largest regional organization of independent producers in the country. Film Arts Foundation, 346 Ninth Street, 2nd Floor, San Francisco, CA 94103. Phone: (415) 552-8760. E-mail: info@filmarts.org. Web site: http://www.filmarts.org.

FILM FINDERS tracks hundreds of independently produced films and publishes information about them in reports that are sold to acquisition executives around the world. You can list your film free of charge in any stage of production. Film Finders, 1024 North Orange Drive, Hollywood, CA 90038. Phone: (323) 308-3489. E-mail: filmfinders@ifilm.com. Web site: http://www.filmfinders.com.

FLASH FORWARD INSTITUTE is an intensive, month-long workshop designed to produce improved career results for people in the entertainment industry. Flash Forward Institute, 2321 West Olive Avenue, Suite A, Burbank, CA 91506. Phone: (323) 850-7392. E-mail: ffinst@aol.com. Web site: http://www.flashforwardinstitute.com.

HOLLYWOOD FILM FOUNDATION awards grants to filmmakers. Projects must have first- or second-time feature director and/or producer and must be budgeted at under $5 million. Hollywood Film Foundation, 433 North Camden Drive, Suite 600, Beverly Hills, CA 90210. Phone: (310) 288-1882. E-mail: info@hff.org. Web site: http://www.hff.org.

INDEPENDENT FEATURE PROJECT (IFP) is a nonprofit organization created to support the work of artists and technicians working in independent film. IFP is organized into five regional locales: New York, Los Angeles, Chicago, Miami, and Minneapolis. Web site: http://www.ifp.org.

INTERNATIONAL DOCUMENTARY ASSOCIATION is the only organization in the United States focusing solely on documentaries and documentarians. It has nearly 2,500 members in 50 countries. International Documentary Association, 1201 West 5th Street, Suite M320, Los Angeles, CA 90017-1461. Phone: (213) 534-3600. E-mail: membership@documentary.org. Web site: http://www.documentary.org.

INTERNET MOVIE DATABASE (IMDb) is an Internet resource for movie fans around the world, containing actor bios, filmographies, credit lists, etc. for just about every film ever made. Web site: http://www.imdb.com.

ORGANIZATION OF BLACK SCREENWRITERS is a nonprofit organization committed to the development and advancement of African American writers. Organization of Black Screenwriters, Inc., P.O. Box 70160, Los Angeles, CA 90070-0160. Phone: (323) 882-4166. E-mail: sswriter@pacbell.net. Web site: http://www.obswriter.com.

SCRIPTWRITERS NETWORK is a volunteer, nonprofit organization of working and aspiring writers, dedicated to providing information and opportunities related to the craft of scriptwriting. Scriptwriters Network, 11684 Ventura Boulevard, Suite 508, Studio City, CA 91604. Hotline: (323) 848-9477. E-mail: info@scriptwritersnetwork.com. Web site: http://www.scriptwritersnetwork.com.

SOCIETY OF COMPOSERS AND LYRICISTS is a nonprofit volunteer organization with a long and distinguished history in the fine art of scoring for motion pictures and television. Society of Composers and Lyricists, 400 South Beverly Drive, Suite 214, Beverly Hills, CA 90212. Phone: (310) 281-2812. Web site: http://www.filmscore.org.

*D*irecting is not just half of you, it's all of you. It's the music
I hear, the colors I see, the experiences that I've had, the people
I've known, the stories that move me. —Jodie Foster